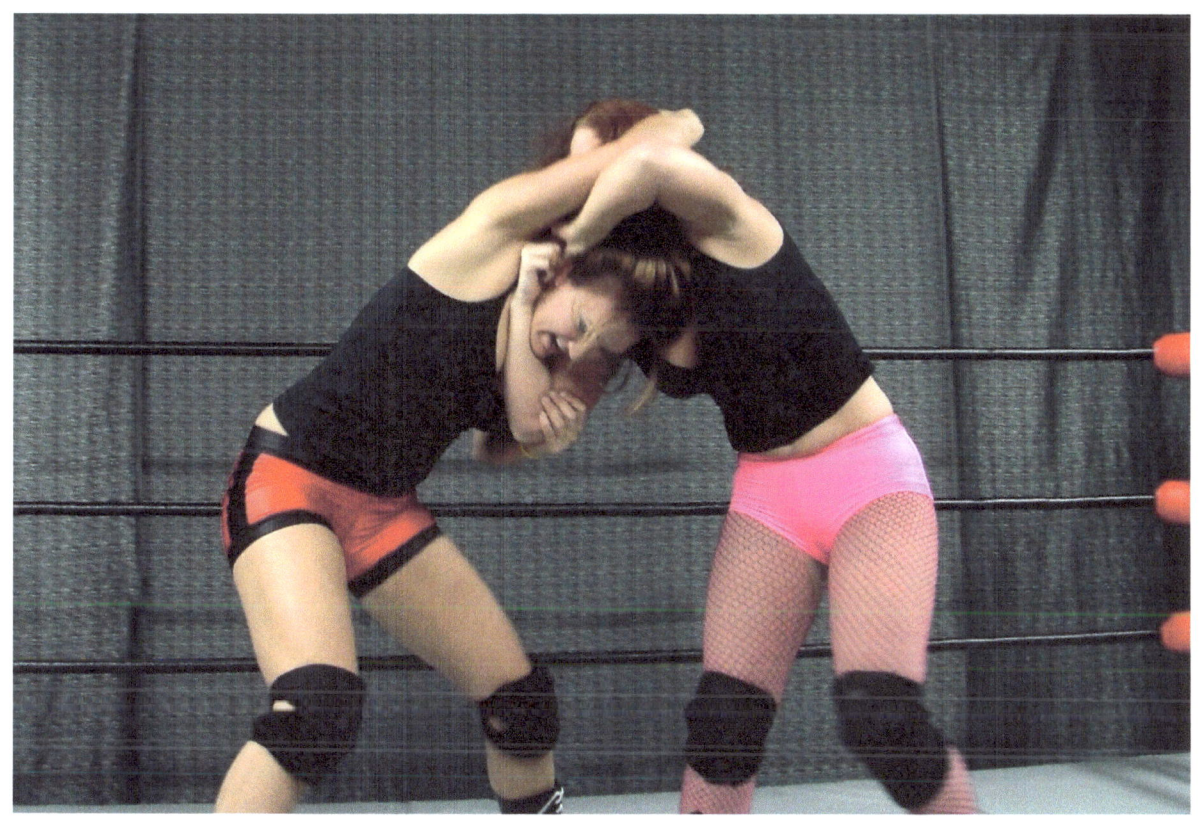

PERILS OF PERSEPHONE

ThunderGirls has always enjoyed sponsoring great wrestlers. Here are four of those girls... one of them, Persephone, featured in three matches. She'll face Madison, Luscious Lee, and Little Jeannie. Not all in one day, of course... though she's probably tough enough to have done it.

Each lady of the ring has their own unique style and personality. Persephone is no exception. Sometimes she's the face, sometimes she's the heel, sometimes it's hard to tell WHICH she is. Her passion and her energy is equal to any wrestler.

Our goal in supporting girls like Persephone and promoting their skills has been merely to let them shine. Persephone does that in these, and all her matches, either at the ThunderGirls gym - or around the world.

Our thanks go to her - and to you, her fans

THUNDERGIRLS MAGAZINE: FALL 2016

Text by: Dayne Adams
Graphic design: Kanban Studio
Photos by: ThunderGirls.com

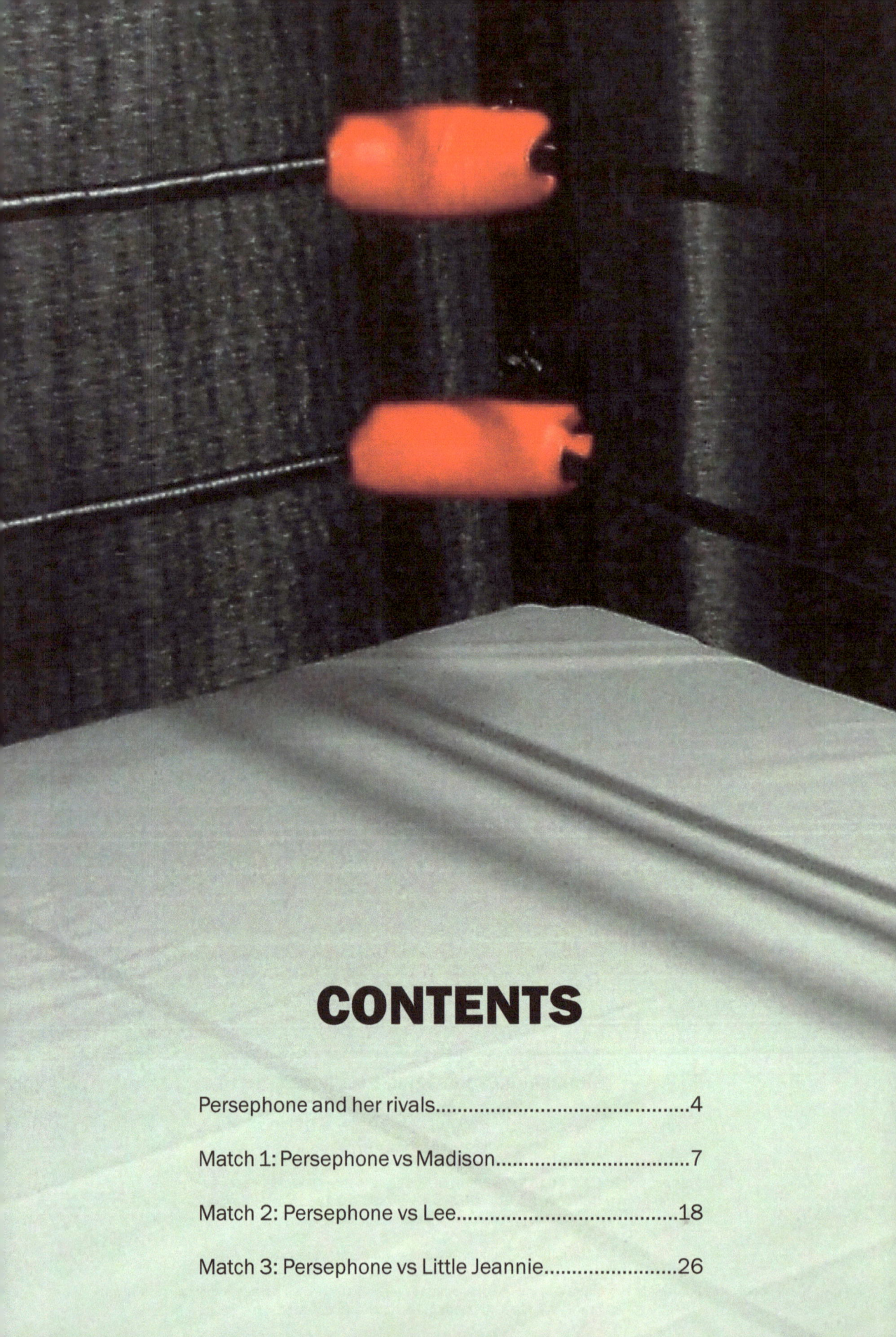

CONTENTS

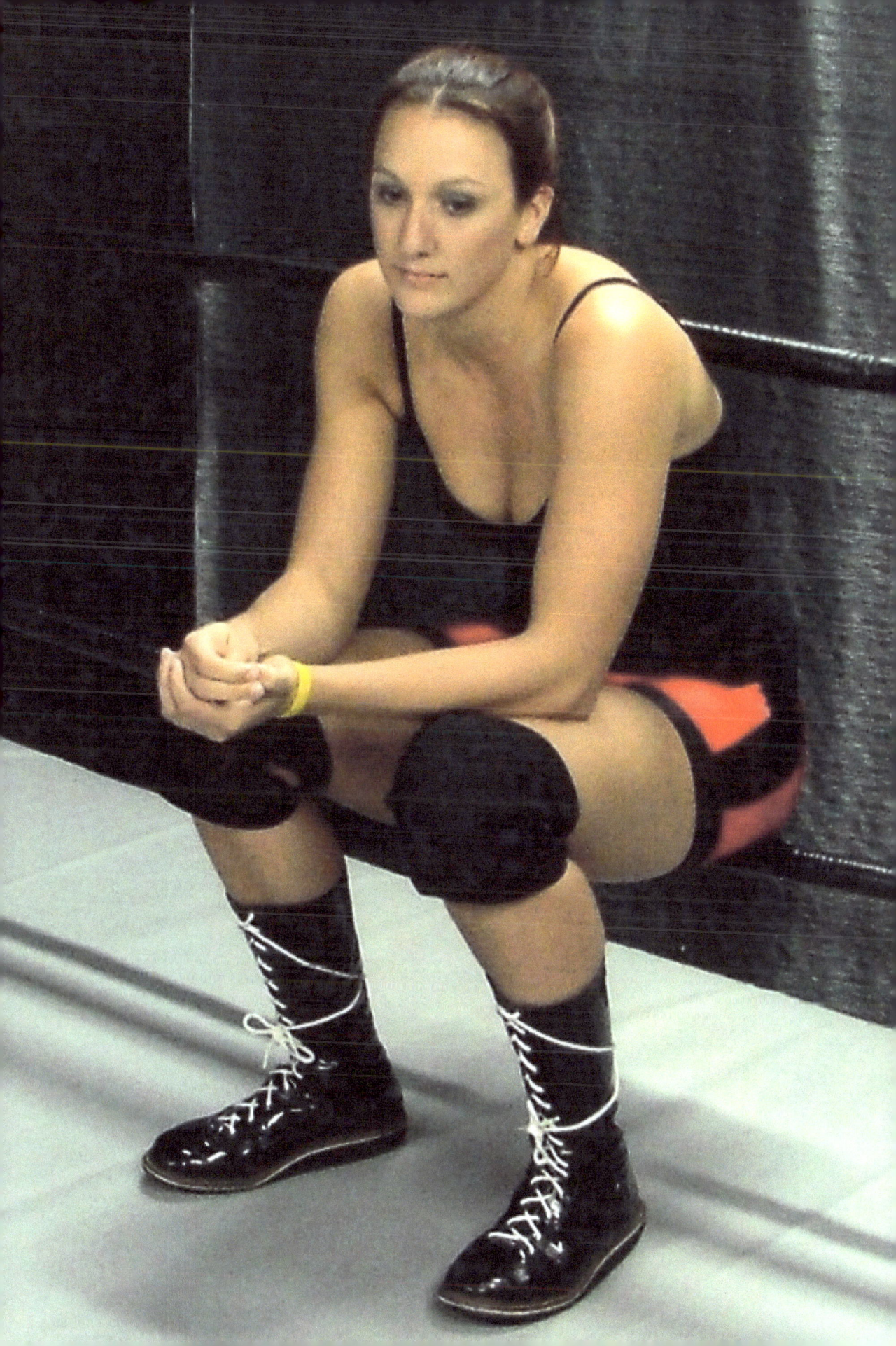

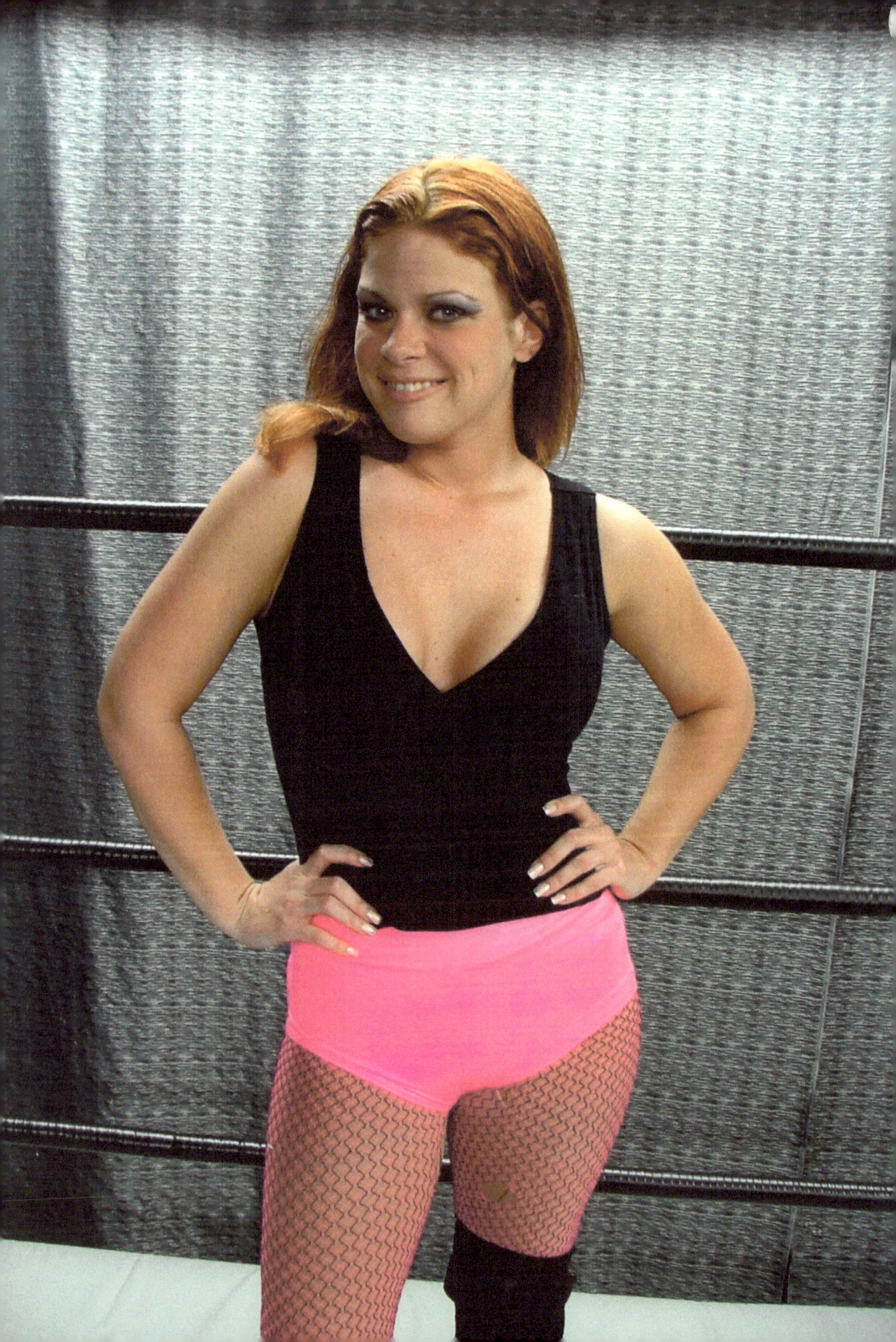

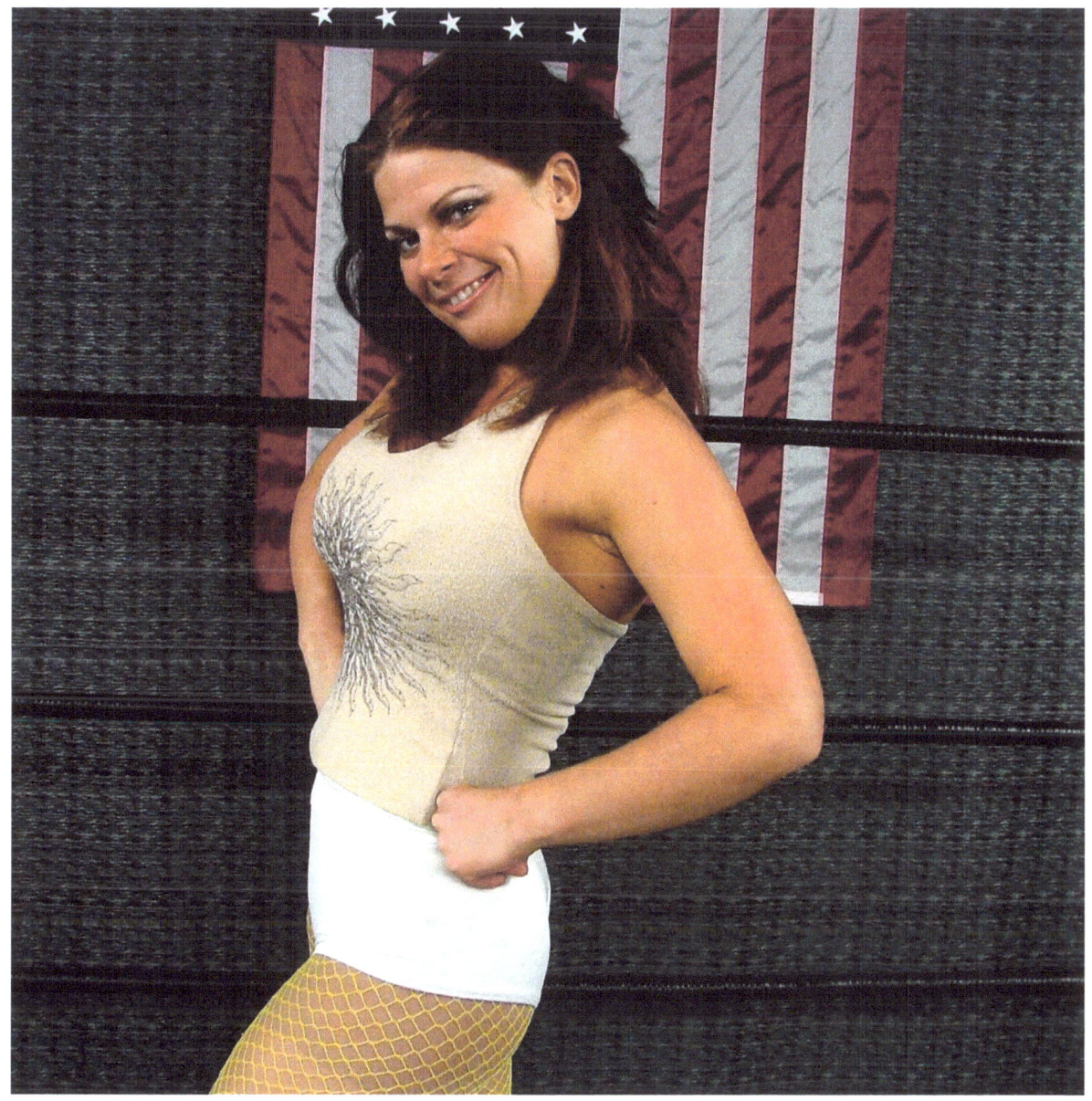

PERSEPHONE

Persophone is one of the great ladies of independent wrestling. Her skills and personality would have fit any decade of female wrestling, or any to come.

Born in Yorktown, Virginia, Persephone has been wrestling since 1999, originally trained byChamp-Pain and Shannon Moore.

This buxom blonde keeps a fairly steady weight of one-hundred forty pounds, which is nicely distributed on her five-foot eight-inch form.

ThunderGirls has been fortunate to book this outstanding girl in most of our live events, and also a number of private video matches as well. Here we present some of her toughest matches, against, of course, some very formidable opponents.

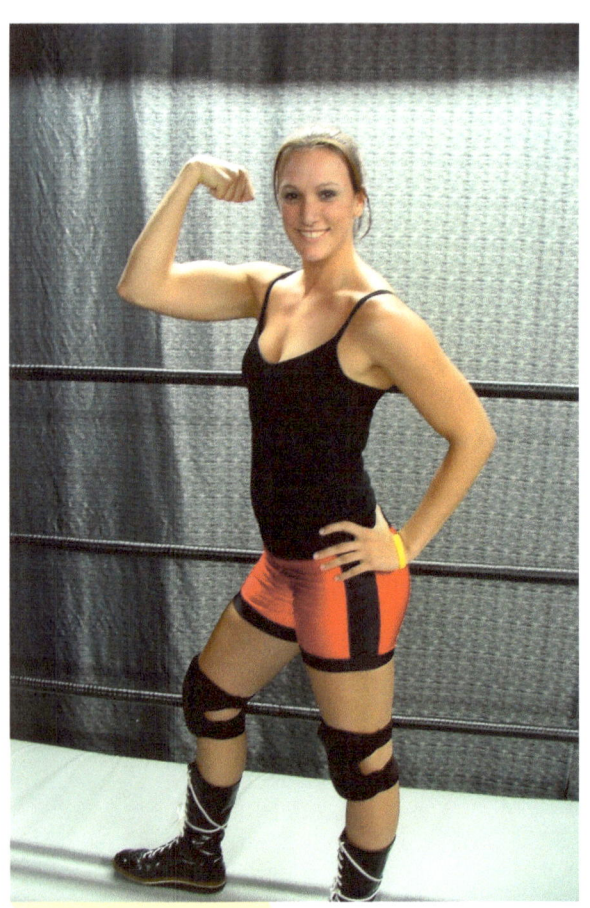

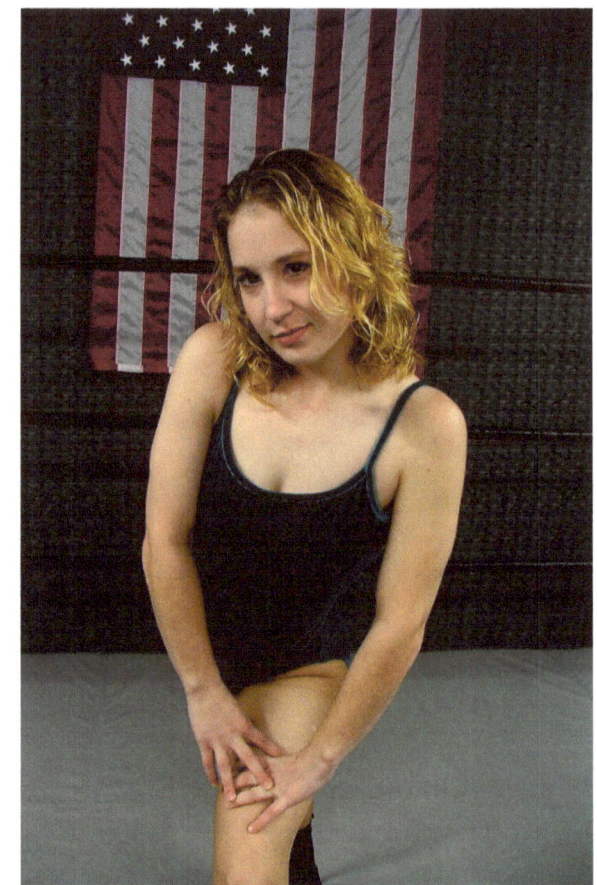

RIVALS

A leggy Australian - a shapely Carolina girl - a buxom New Yorker. What have they in common?

Each of them takes on rough and tumble Persephone in this issue of ThunderGirls Magazine.

Persephone has wrestled in cards all over the country, but three of her toughest matches took place right here in the ThunderGirls ring. Each of these rivals is a different size and has a different style of wrestling. Persephone will have her work cut out for her to leave the ring victorious.

Win or lose, we know you will enjoy watching the action unfold in these

PERILS of PERSEPHONE!

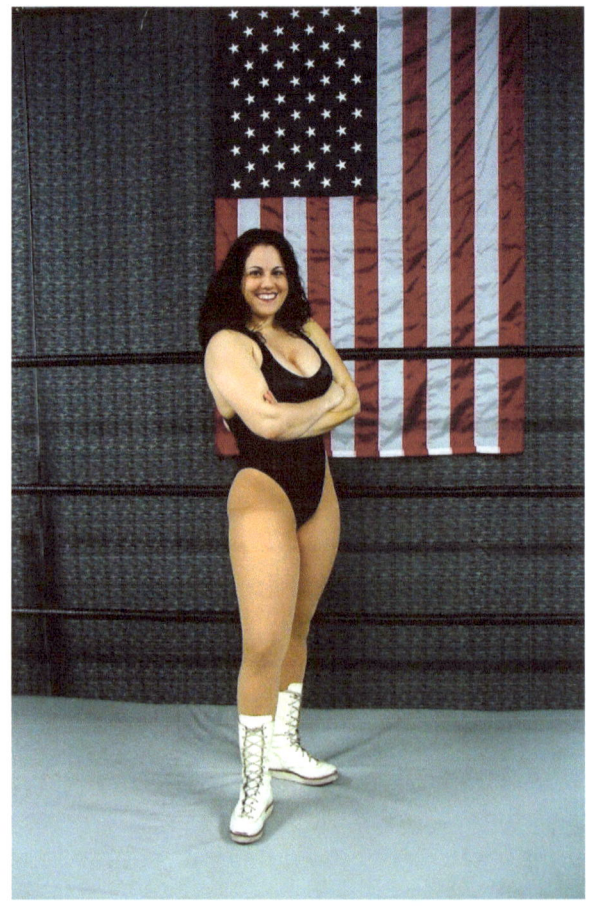

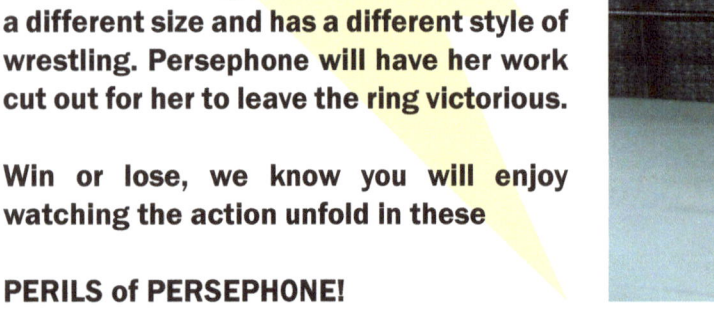

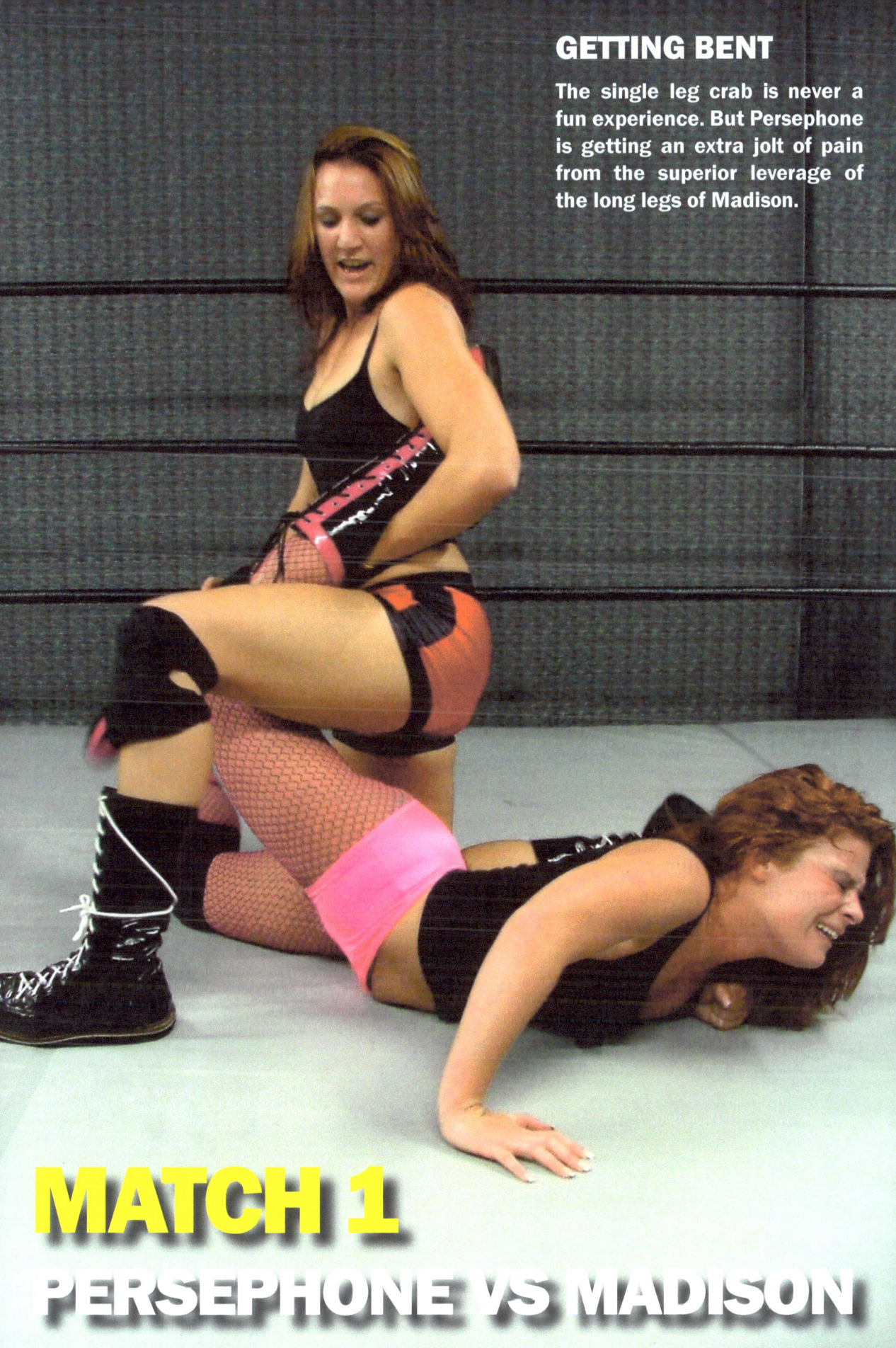

GETTING BENT

The single leg crab is never a fun experience. But Persephone is getting an extra jolt of pain from the superior leverage of the long legs of Madison.

MATCH 1
PERSEPHONE VS MADISON

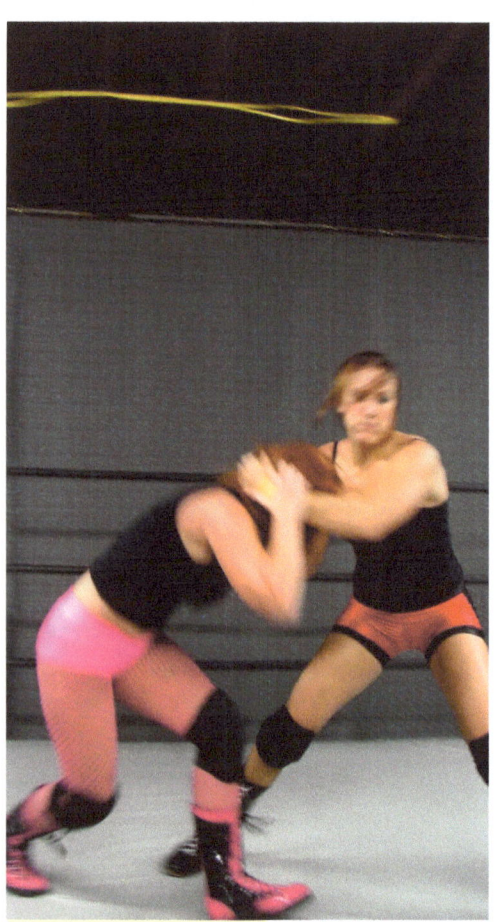
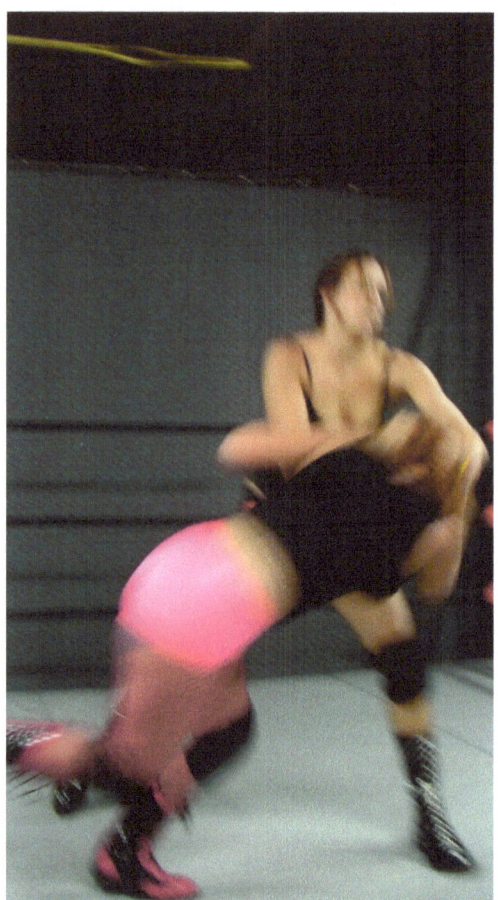
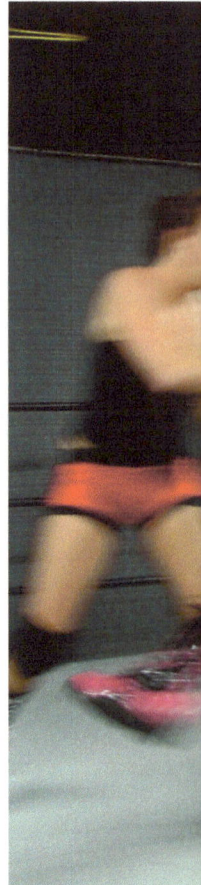

FROM THE OPENING BELL...

Madison went right after Persephone, tossing her around the ring and trying to stomp her into submission.

A little soon for that...

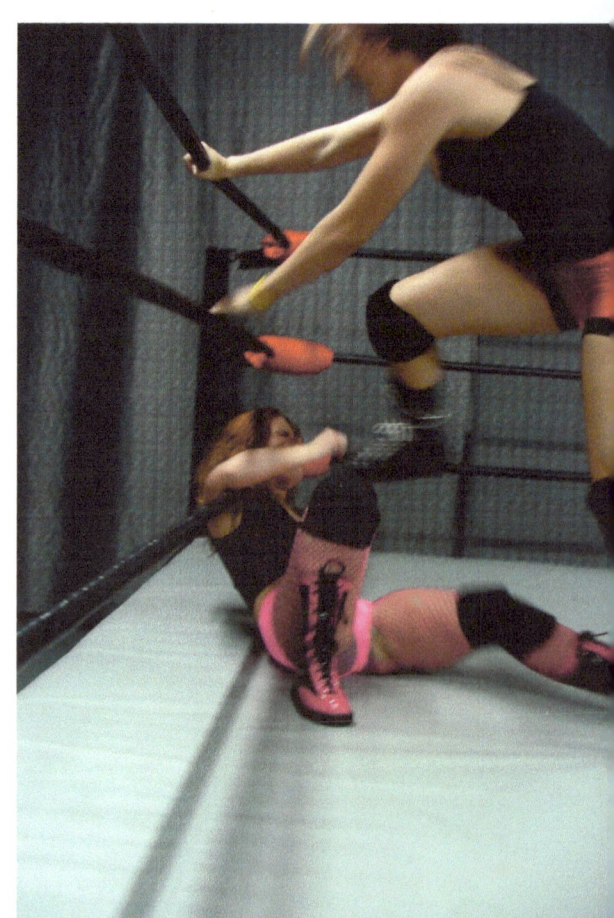

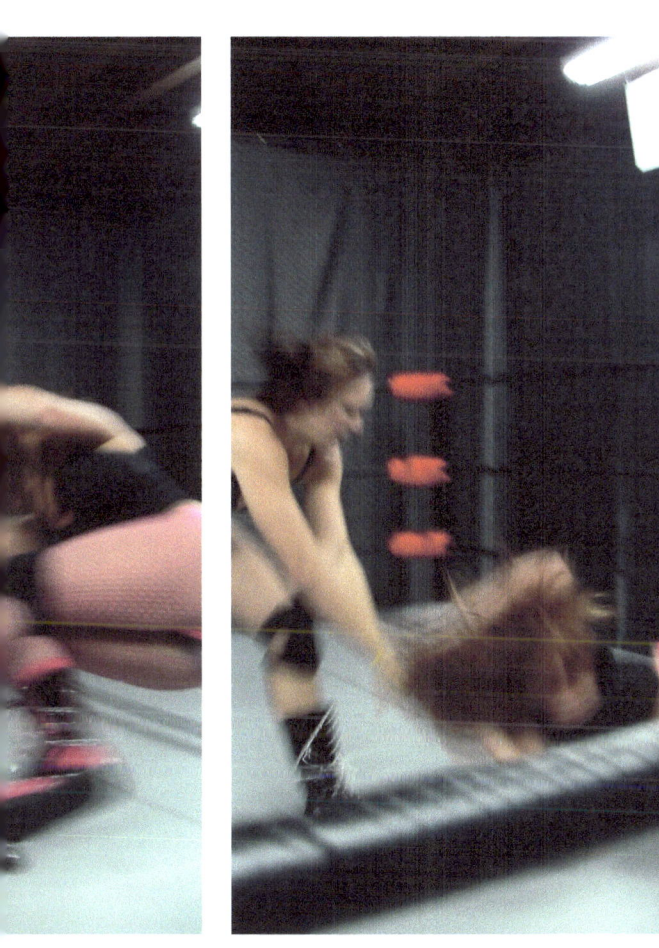
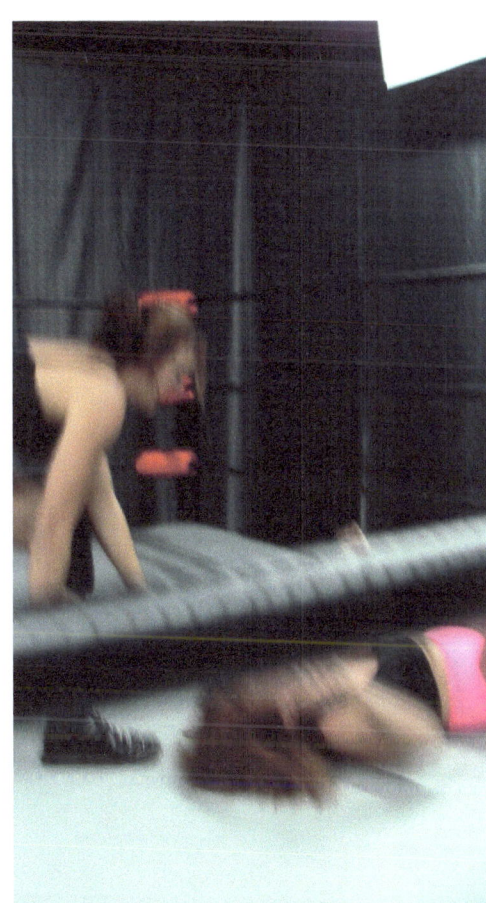
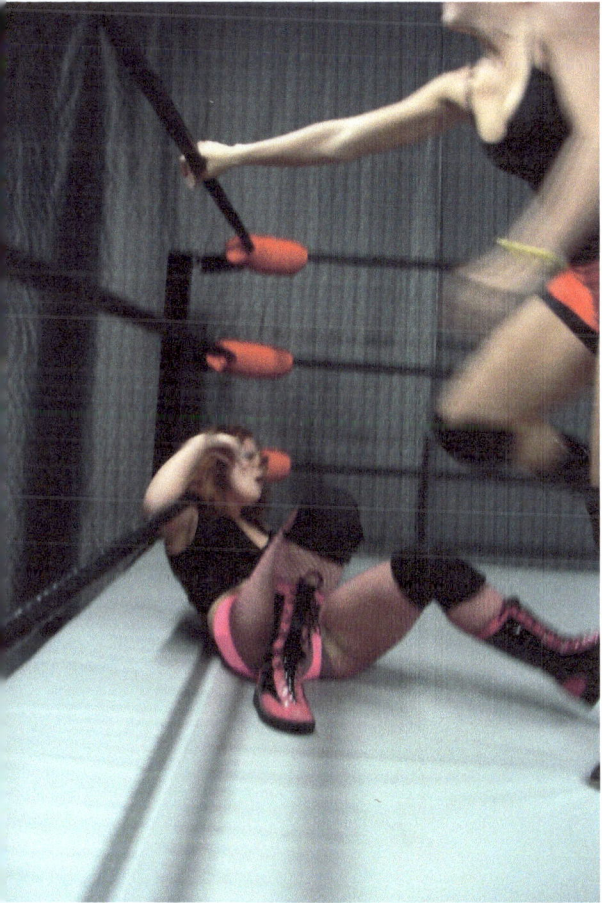
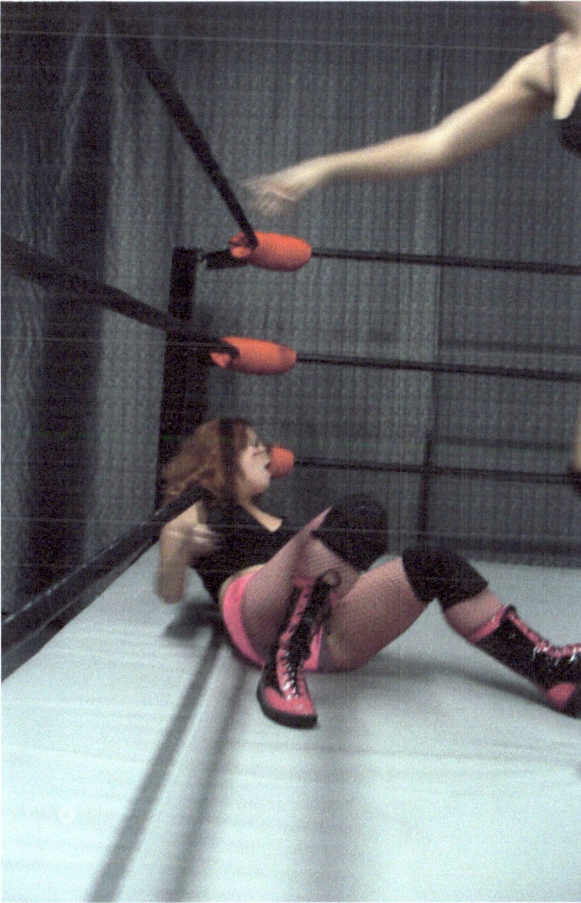

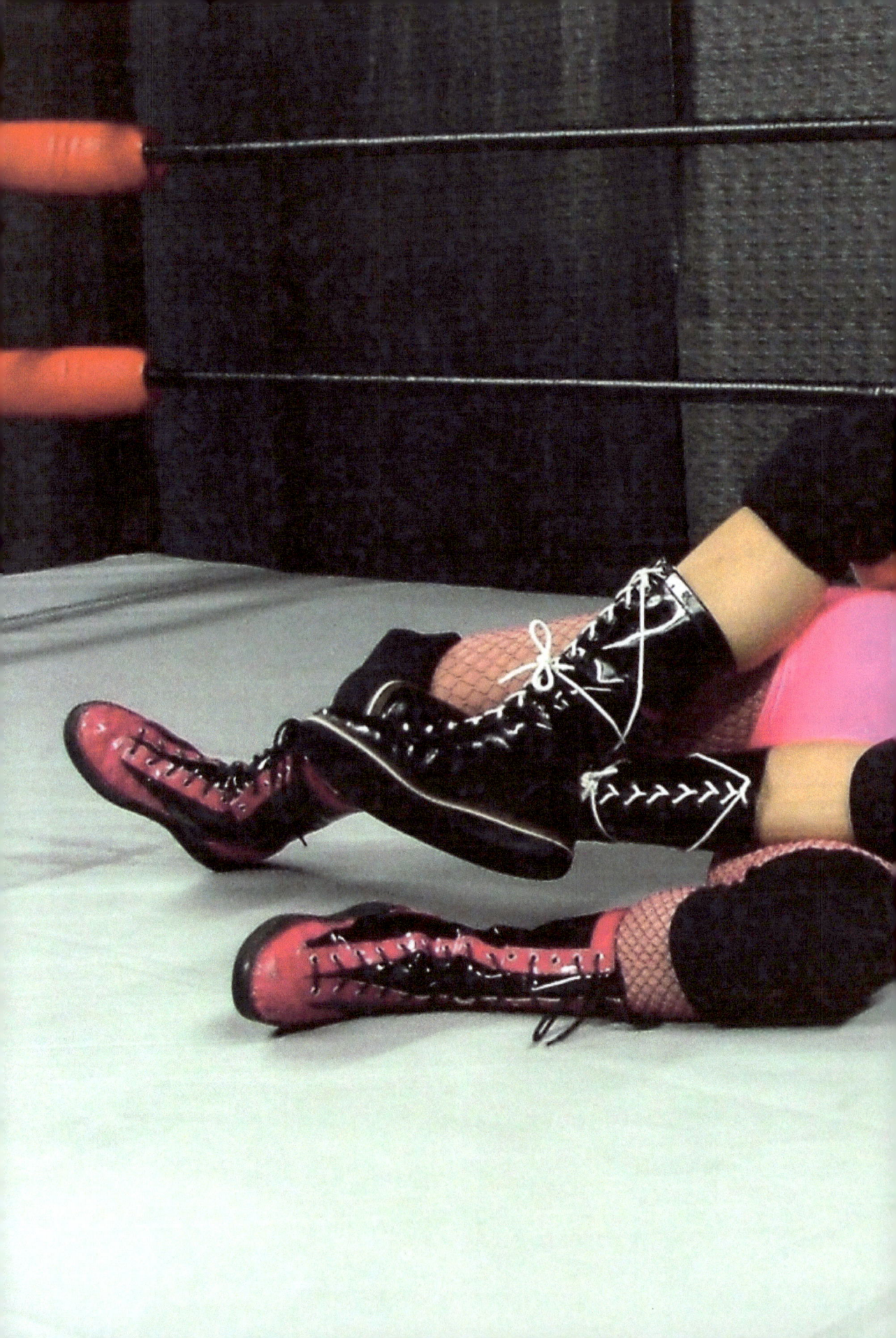

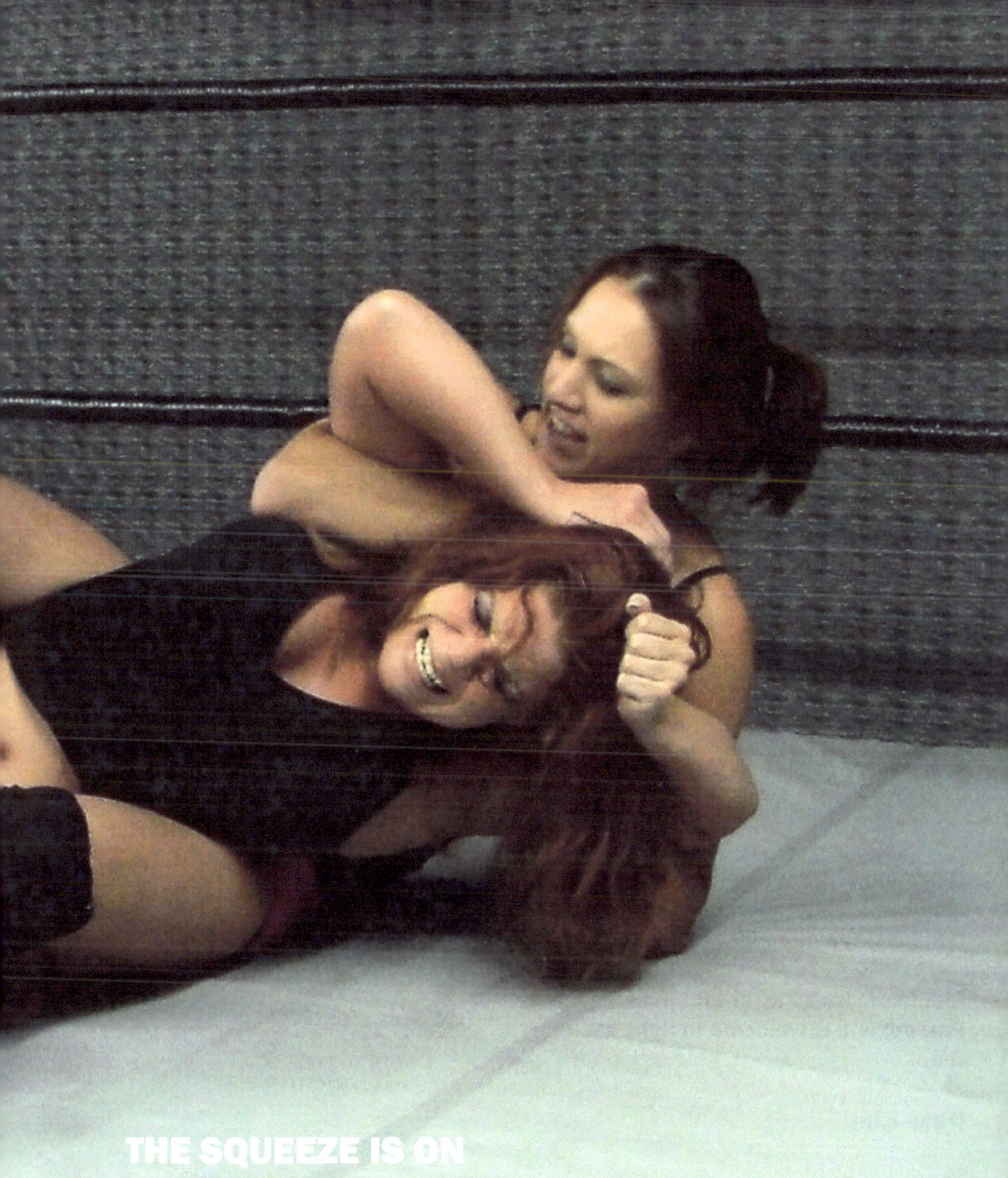

THE SQUEEZE IS ON

We wrestling fans do love to see the scissors in action. Even a small girl can inflict pain on her opponent when she gets her ankles locked around an opponent. But how about a long-legged wrestler?

Archimedes once said something about "Give me a lever long enough..."

I wonder what he'd say about a wrestler who has "long enough?"

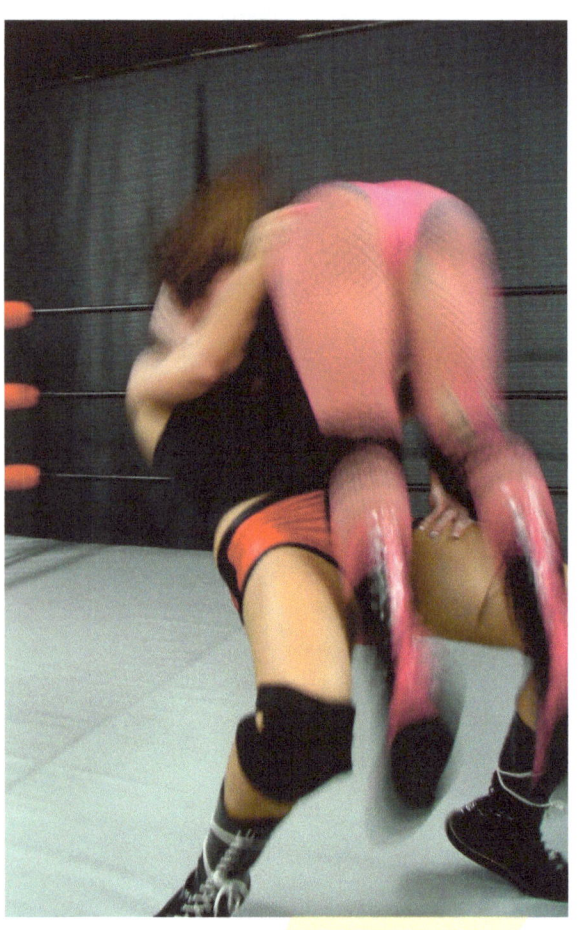

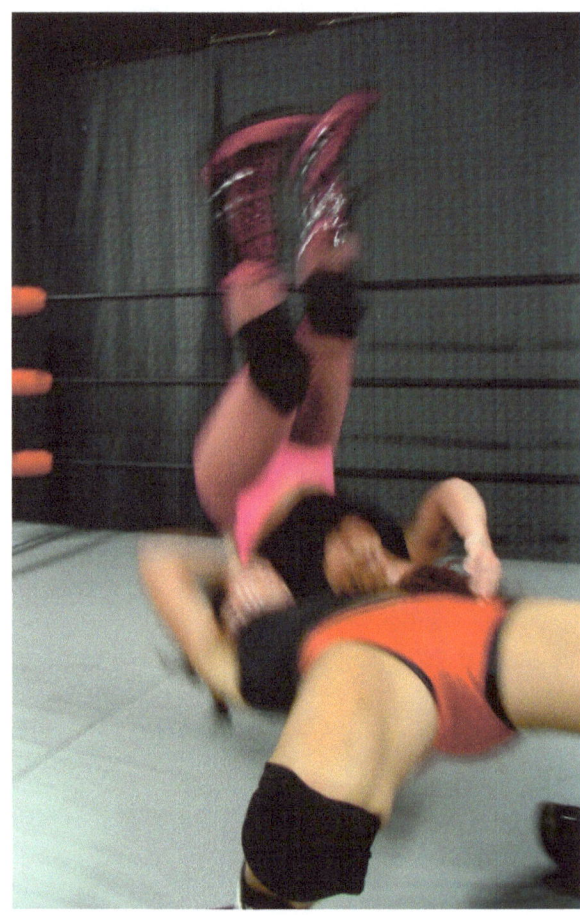

UP, UP, AND OVER

It has to get old, being the victim in a one sided wrestling match. Or should we call it a punishment bout?

Madison isn't a cruel wrestler, and Persephone is welcome to fight back any time.

If she can!

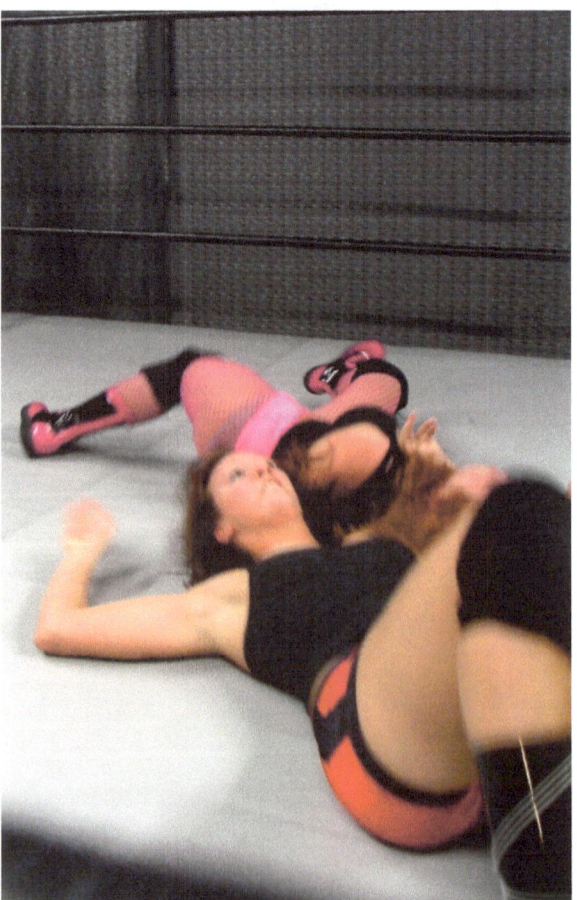

NOT OUT OF THE FIGHT

As with most humans, don't back us into a corner. Persephone does get tired of being treated like a rag doll, and the fire comes out of the redhead.

For a while, anyway...

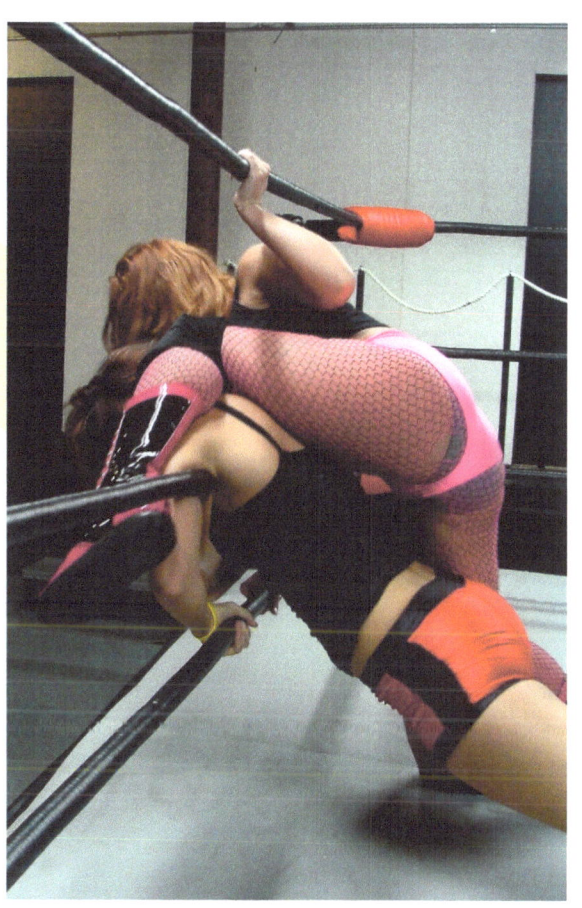

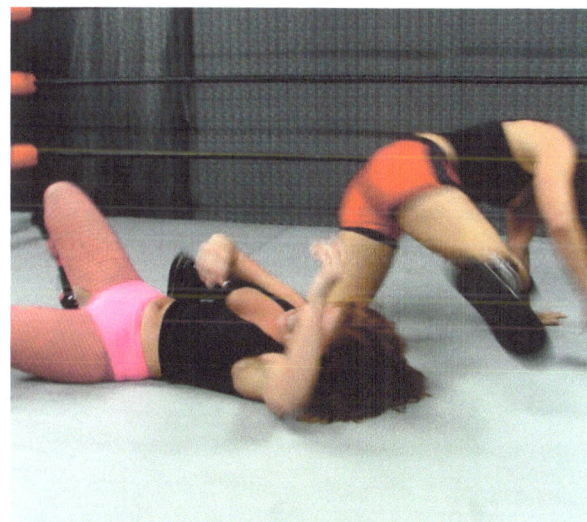

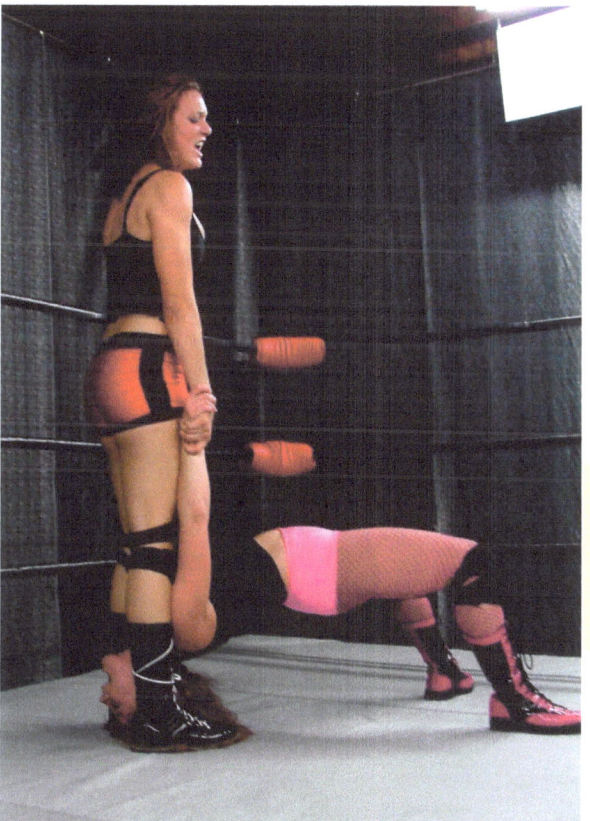

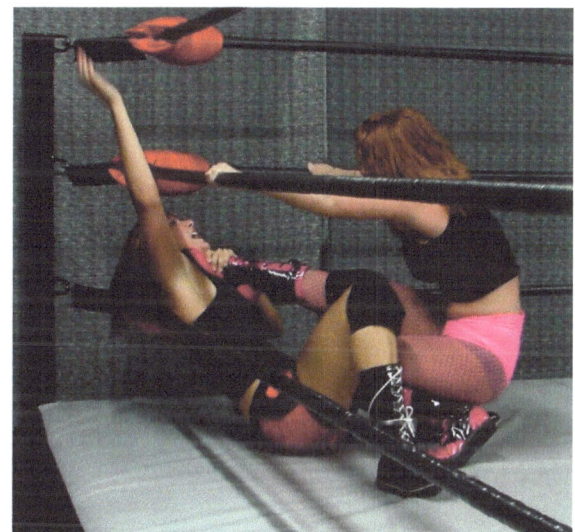

FEET MATTER

Though it's called wrestling, there is a generous use of feet (and boots) in a bout. They can be used to kick or choke, or (left) with some ingenuity, even pull hair.

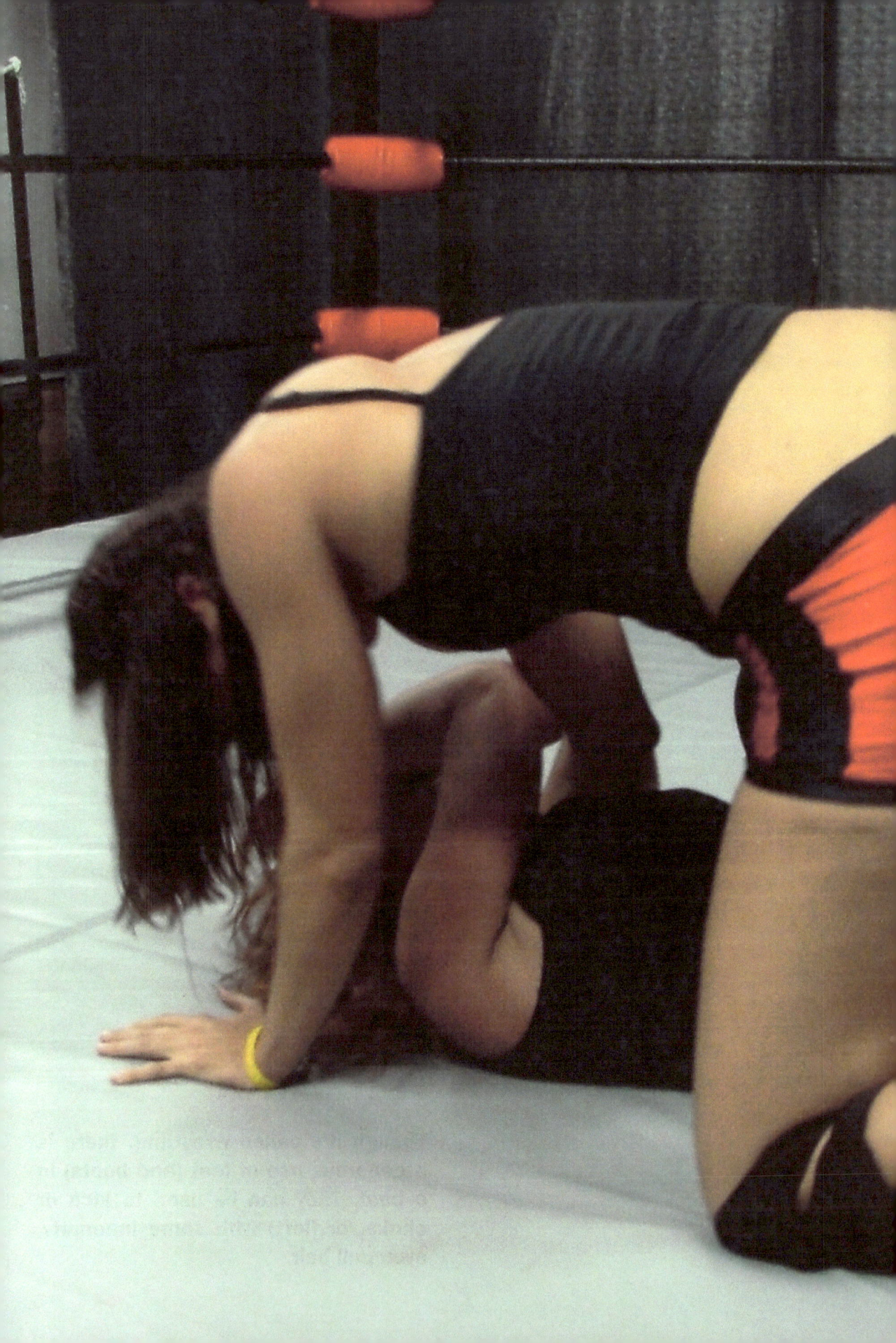

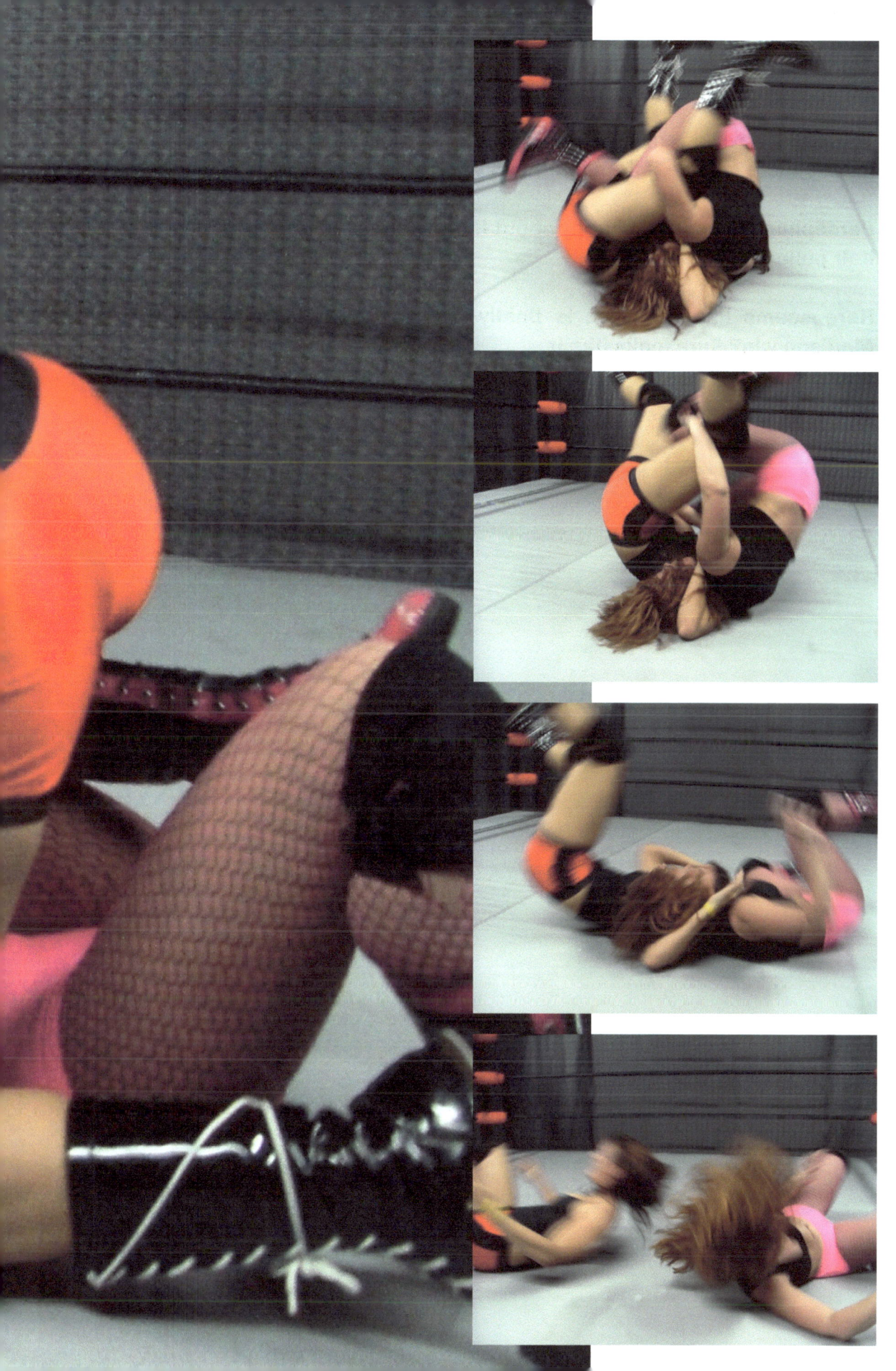

HAIR, REF!

You can't have a wrestling match with women unless there's some hair pulling, can you?

Persephone is none too happy about it being her hair pulled.

Here seems like the bout is finally over. Did Madison win? Sure looks like it.

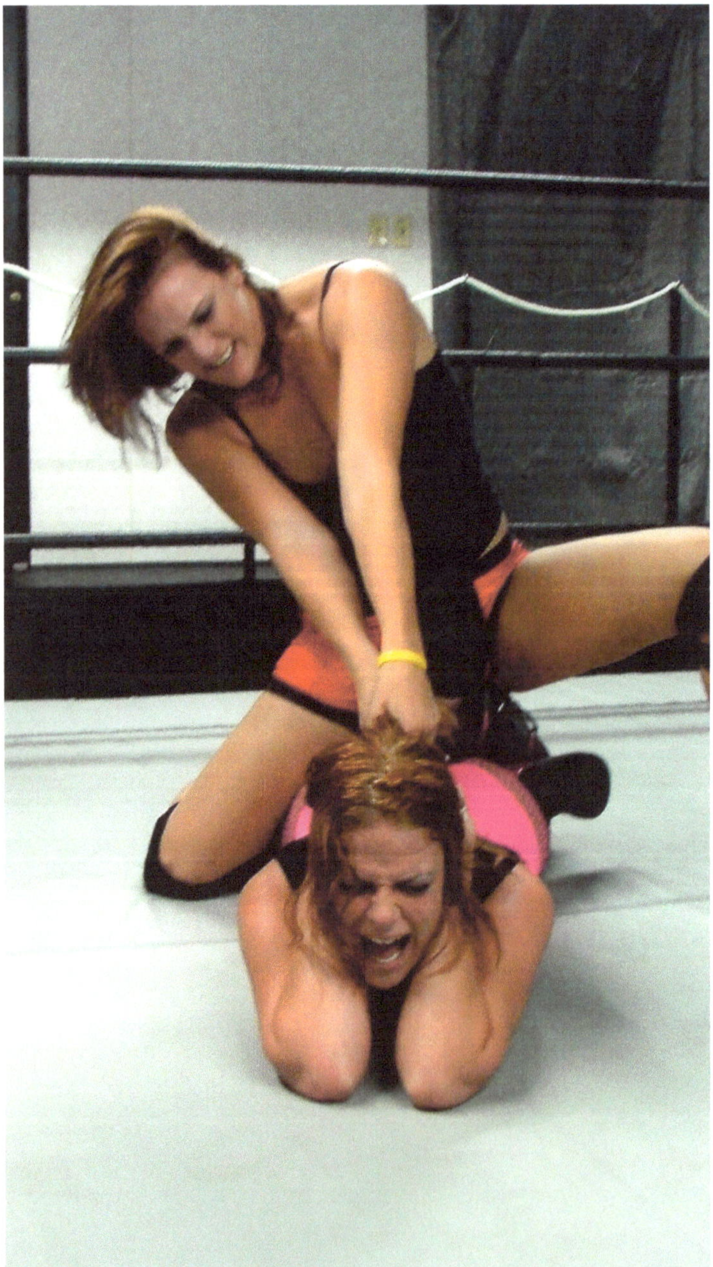

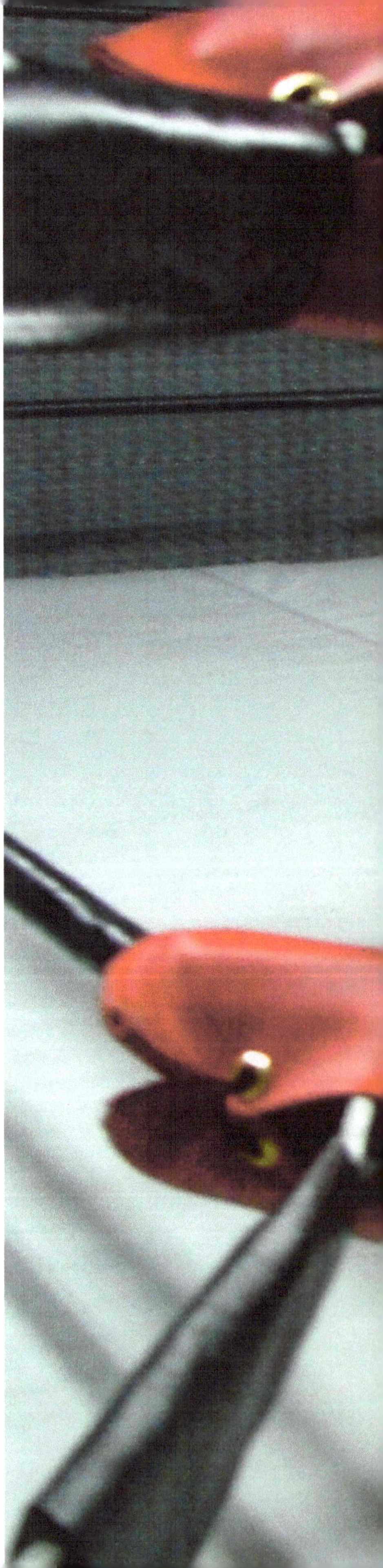

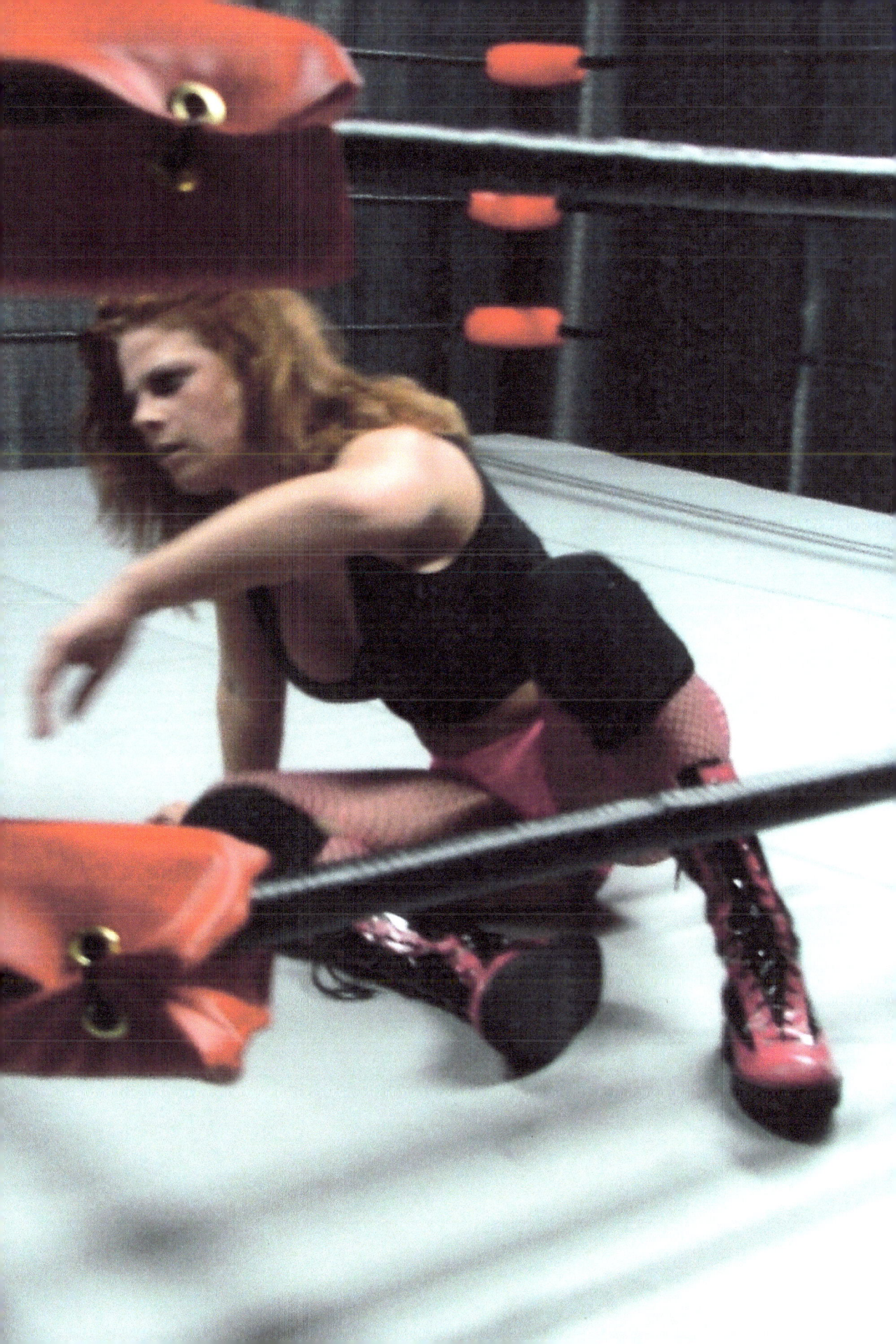

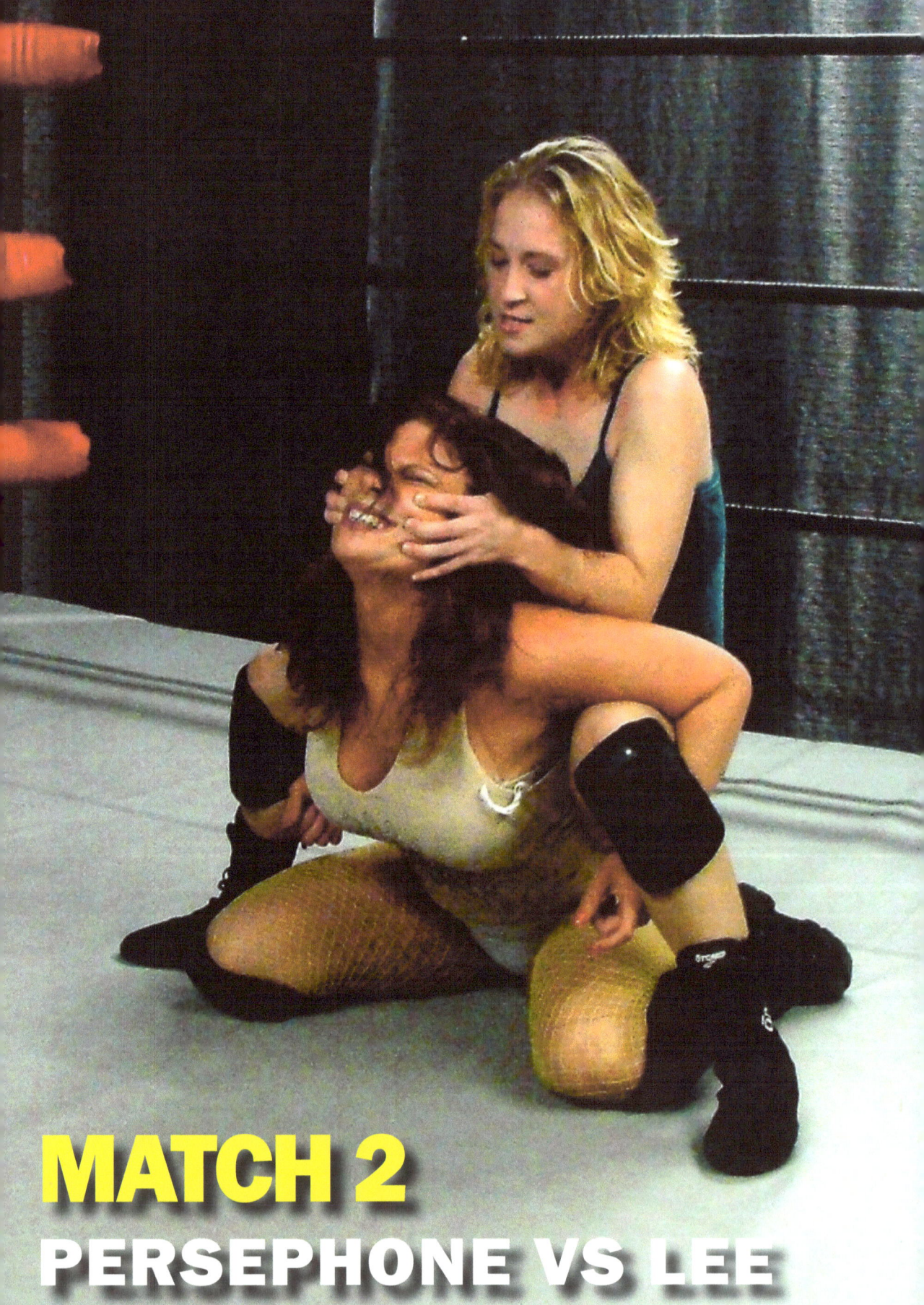

MATCH 2
PERSEPHONE VS LEE

LUSCIOUS LEE

The blonde spitfire known as Luscious Lee was the second "ThunderGirl" to join us. She actually started training at the age of 17, just a couple of weeks before her first match against the Rowdy Redhead, Becca.

Lee was a short girl, but athletic and determined. She took to wrestling like a duck to water, and while she was known to lose a few matches, she also won many that no one - especially her opponents - expected.

Lee didn't keep up with the outside world of pro wrestling, and so she didn't know the reputation Persephone had on the circuit. The bigger girl was usually known to play fair (barely) but often used power moves to stun her opponent, then toying with them like a cat and a mouse.

Lee was nobody's mouse.

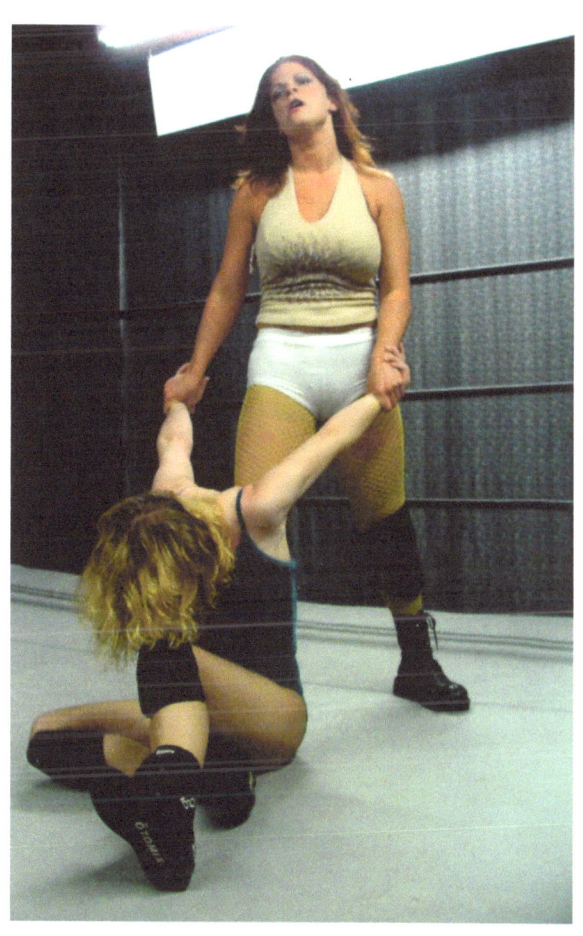

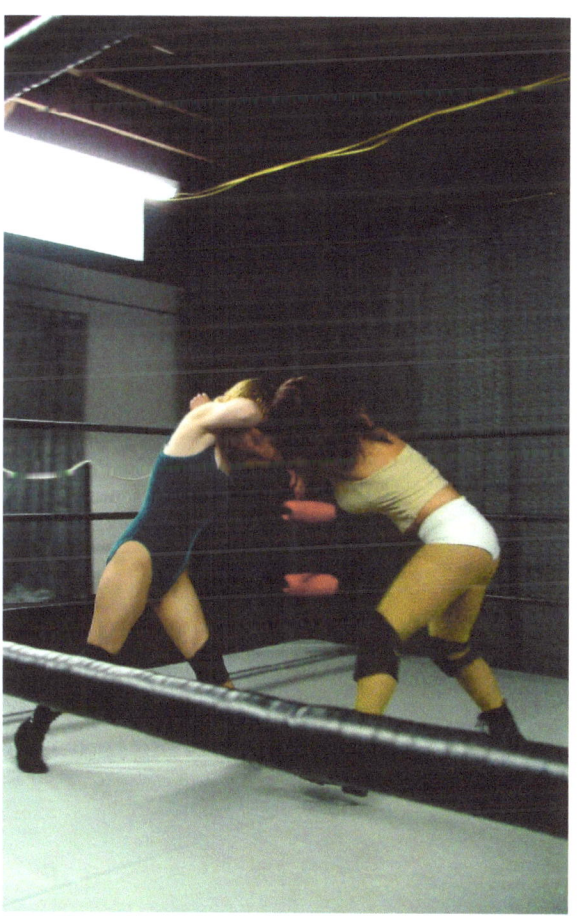

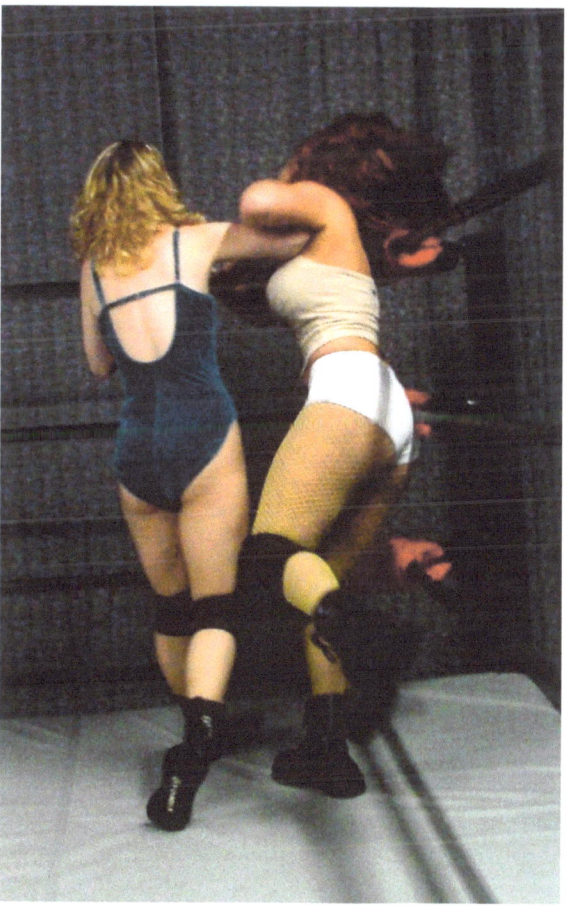

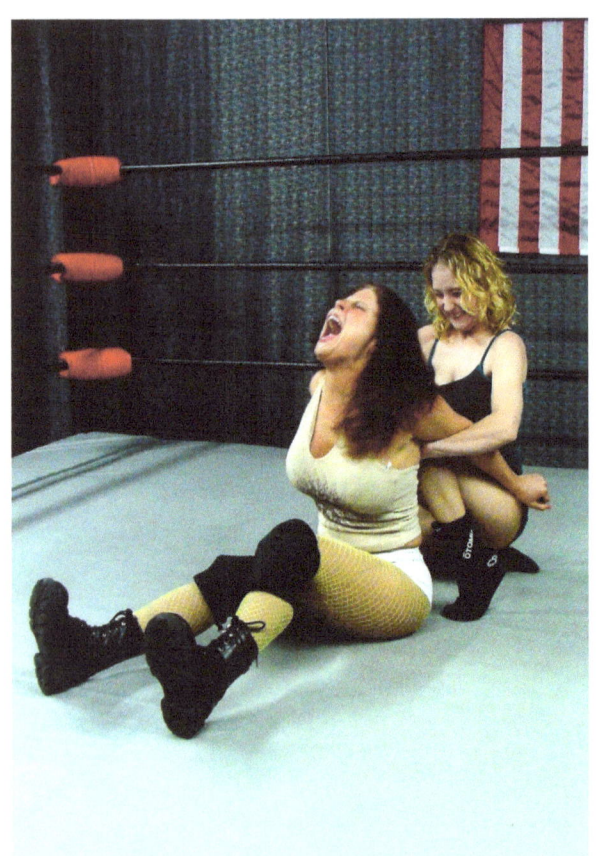

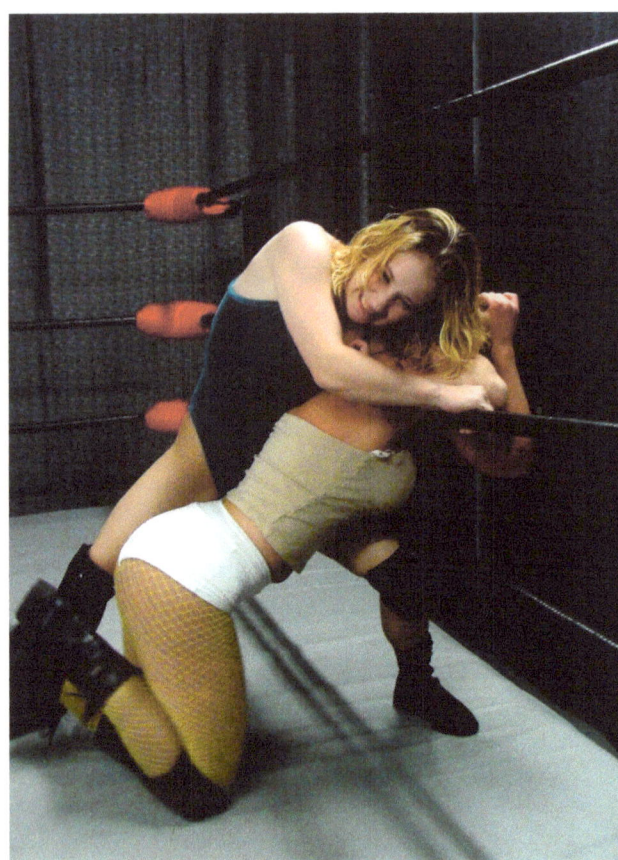

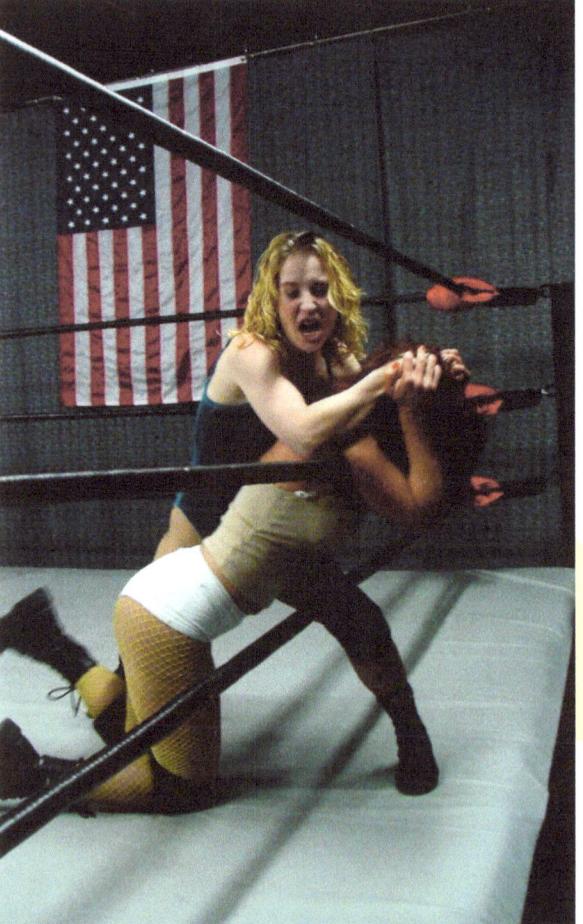

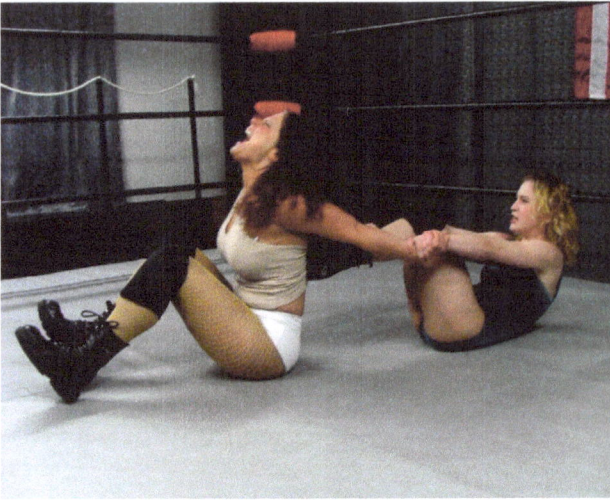

WHODDATHUNKIT?

Persephone is bigger and arguably badder, but our Luscious Lee seems to be having her way with the big redhead.

TURN ABOUT

Persephone didn't let Lee work her over for long, and now the blonde is on the receiving end of some redheaded wrestling fury.

Not the first time... won't be the last.

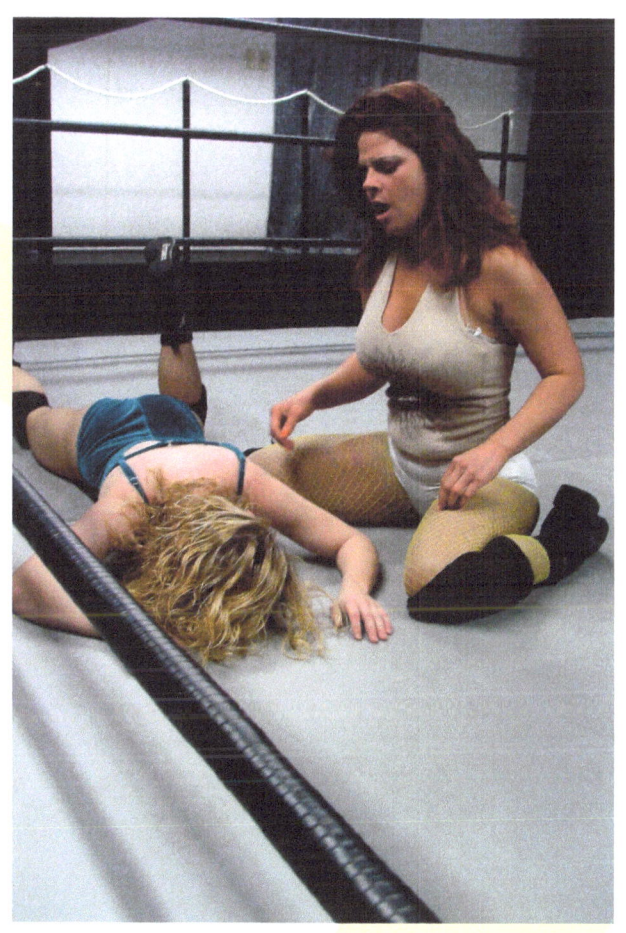

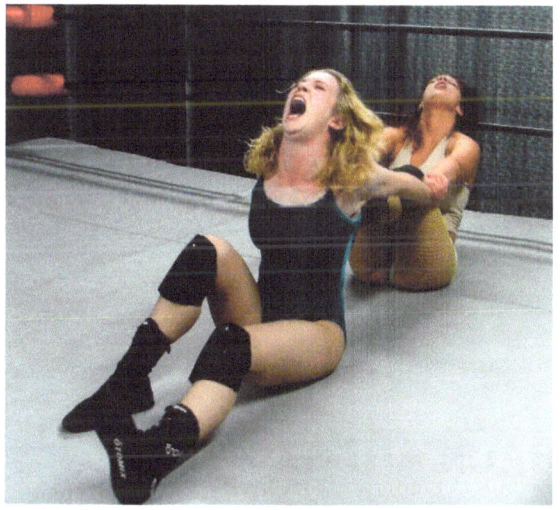

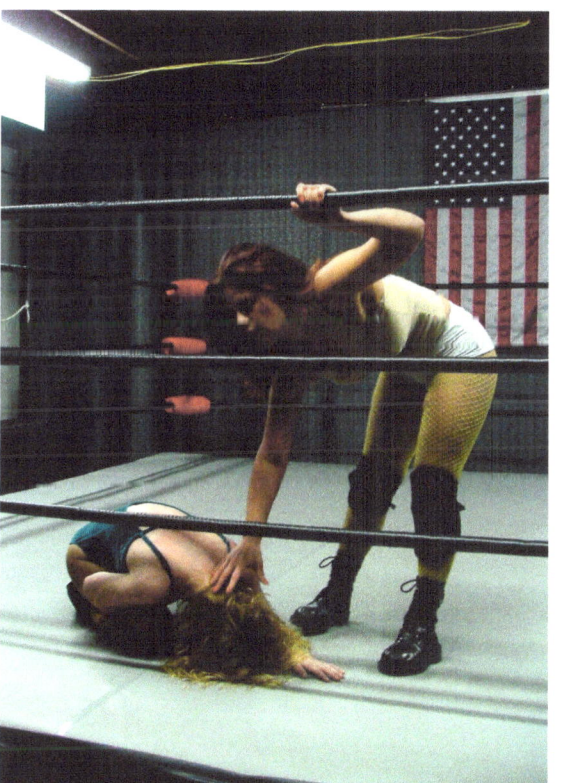

TAUNTING

A wrestler's ego is is part of why they step in the ring in the first place. When they have control over their opponent, they like to brag.

Sometimes not a good idea.

Luscious Lee may be down...

...but she's not OUT!

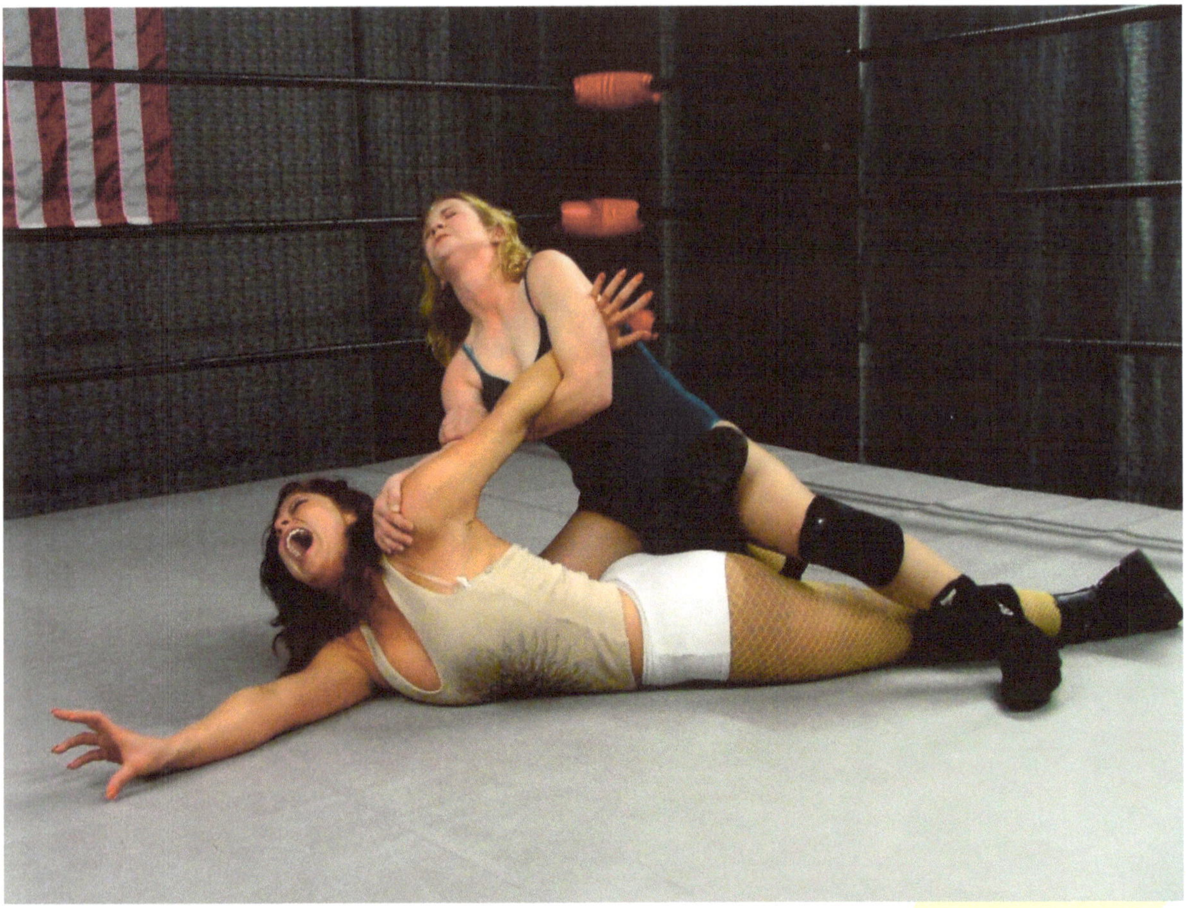

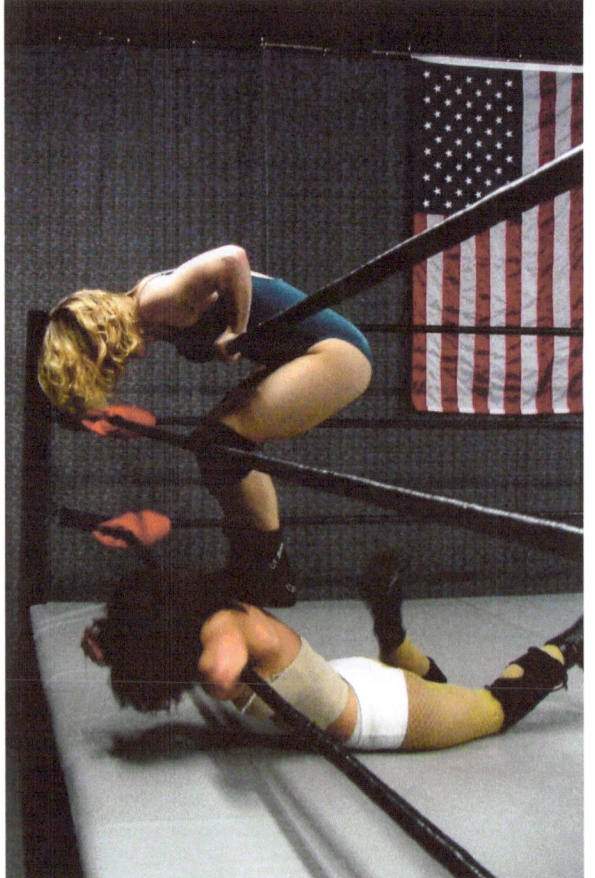

BACK AND FORTH

Now these beautiful young wrestlers have gotten the measure of each other, and they are a little more cautious, a little more methodical. This gives us a great, measured bout where we get to see more of their true wrestling skills.

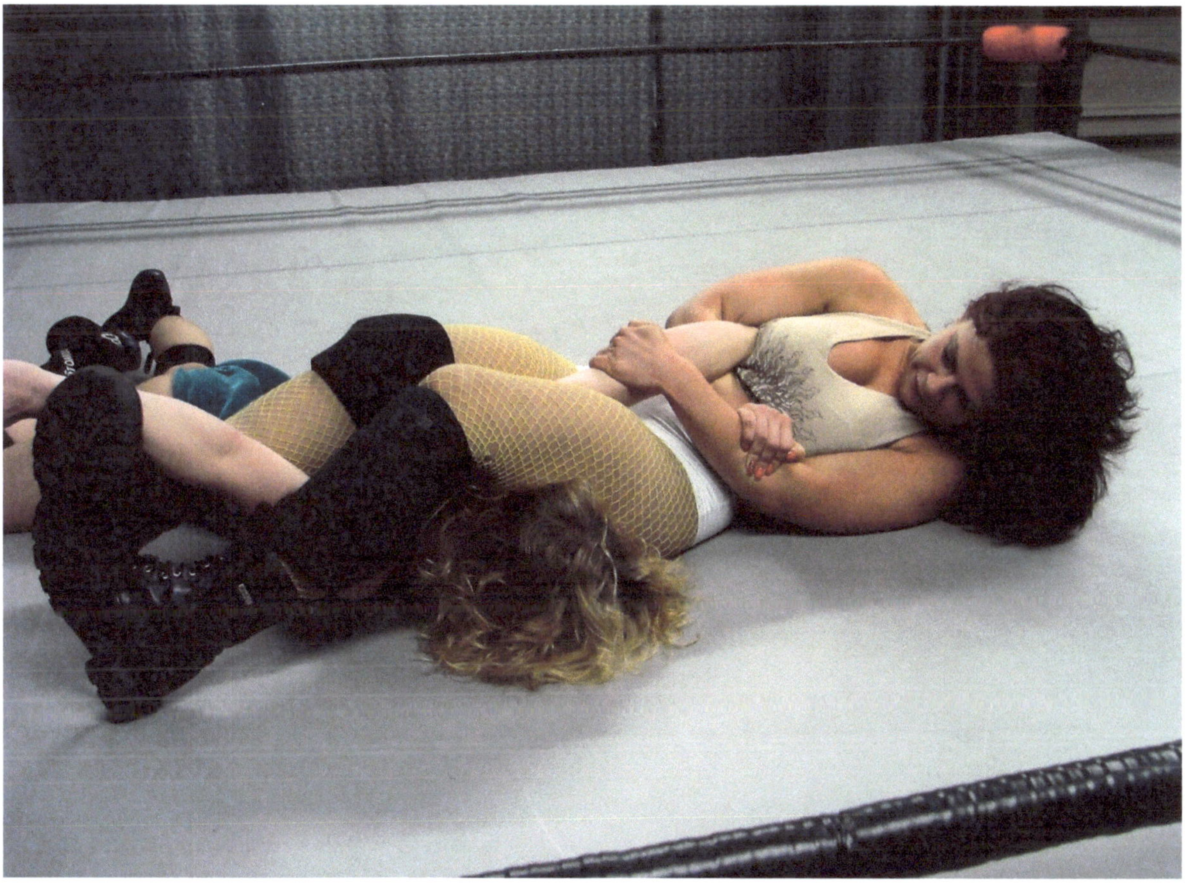

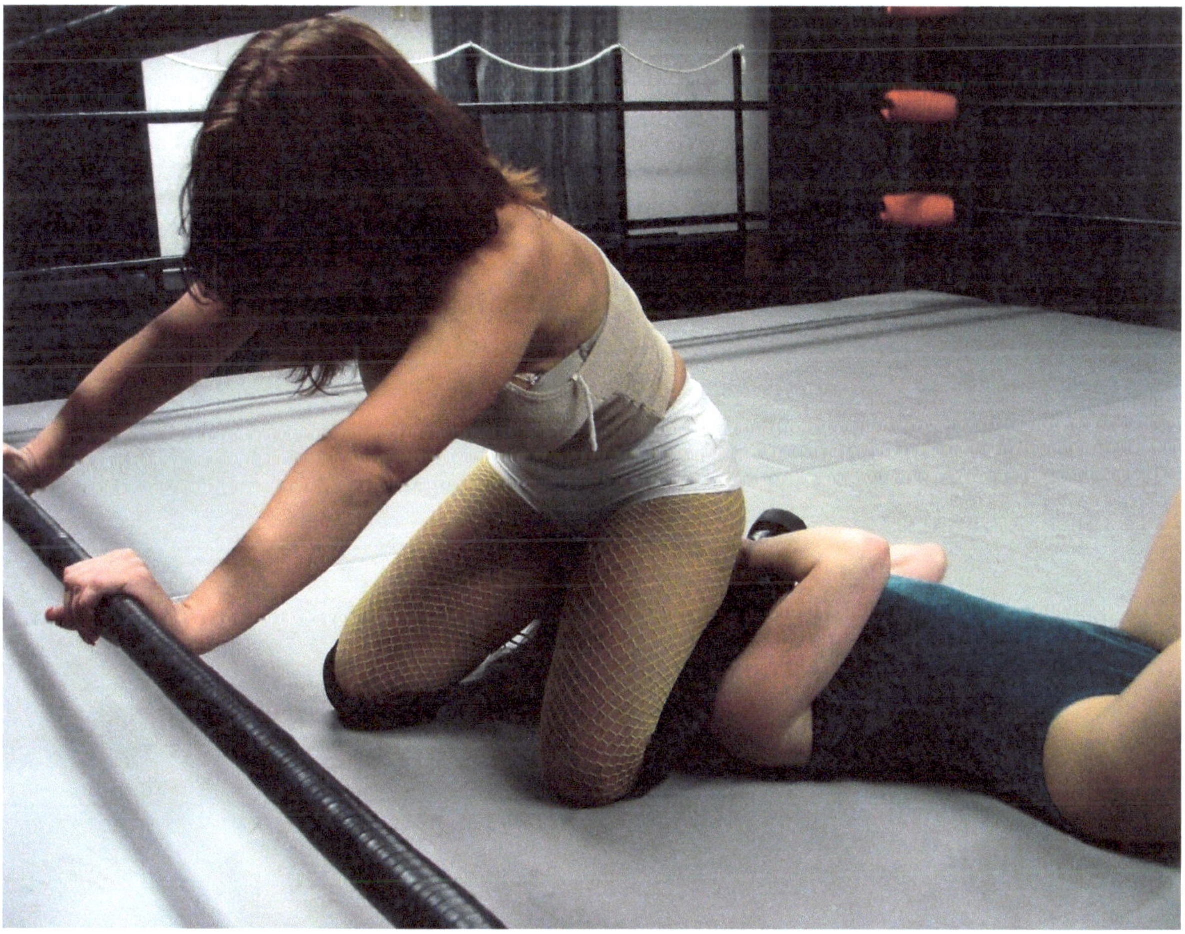

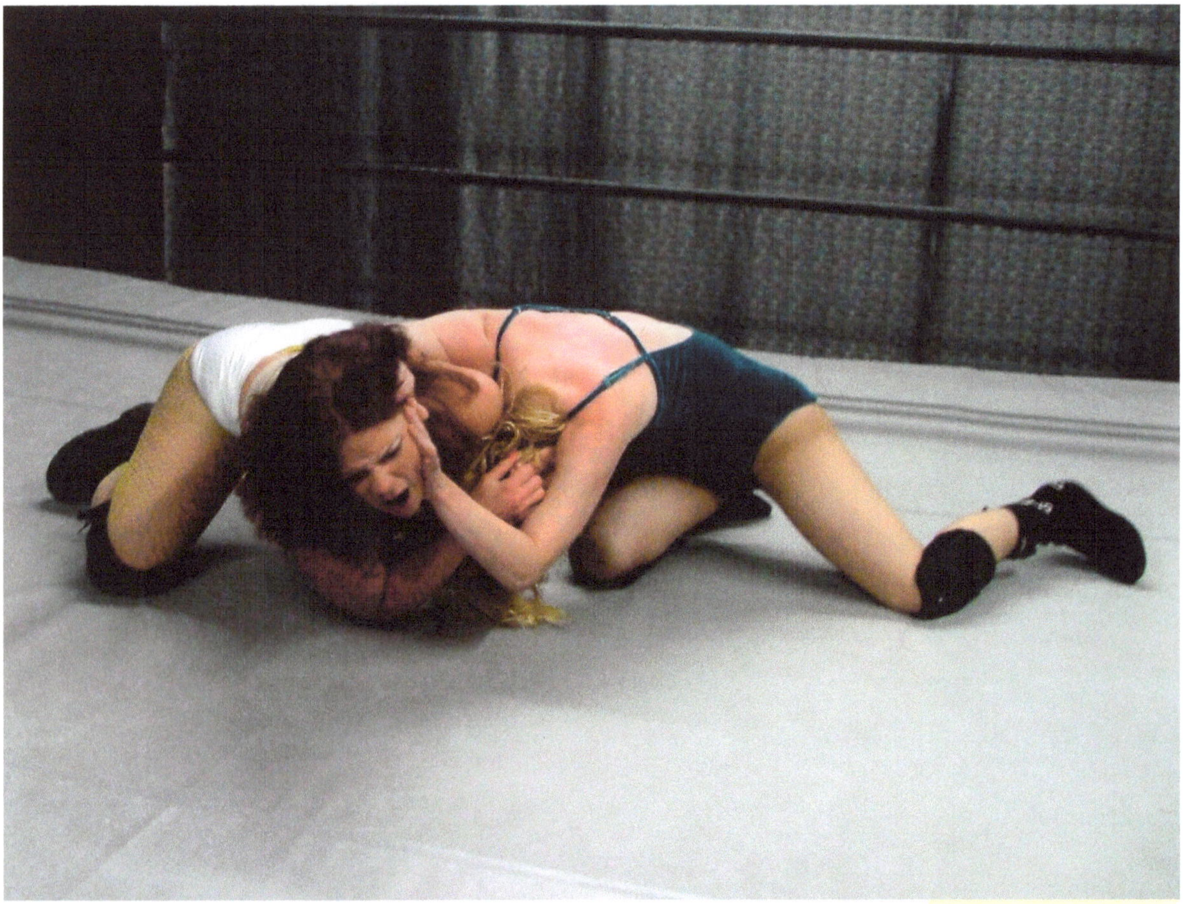

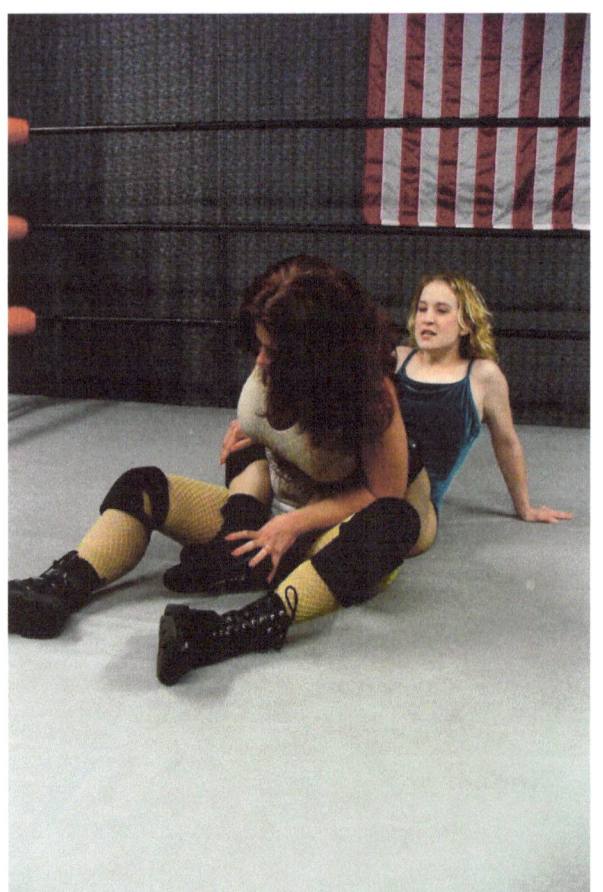

HAIR, AGAIN...
AND OTHER THINGS!

Supposedly "fur flying" refers to animals like cats in battle. Well it applies to girls wrestling, too. The girls seek to hurt and control the other, and they seem to be doing a mighty fine job of it.

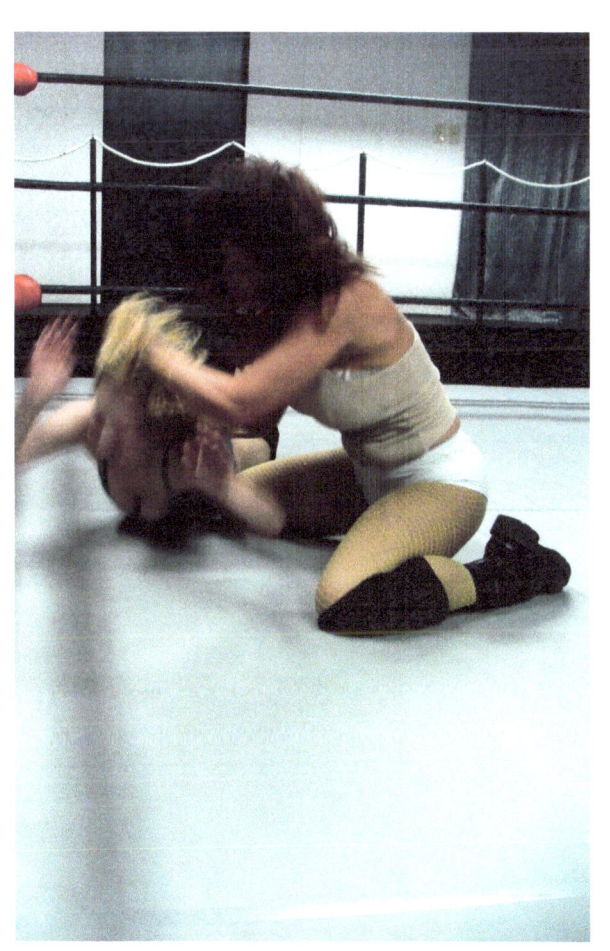
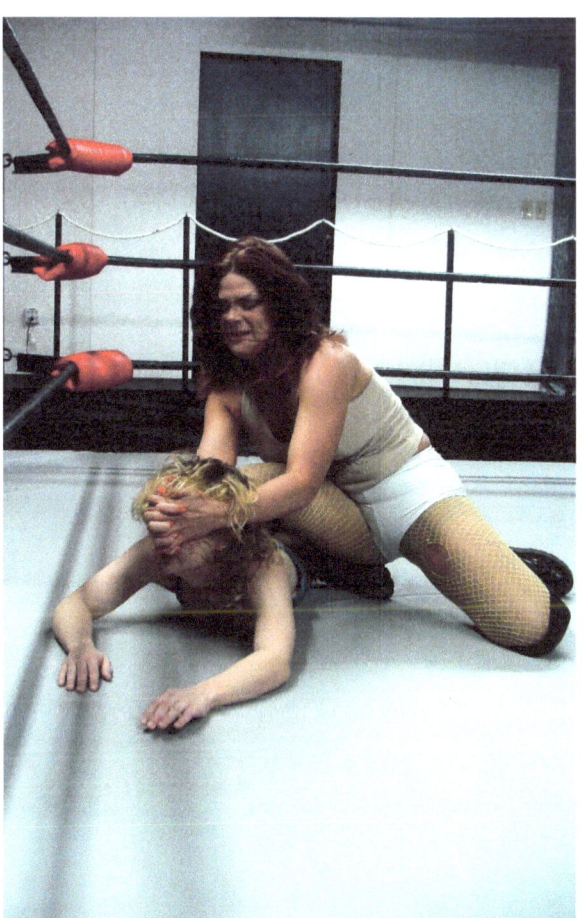

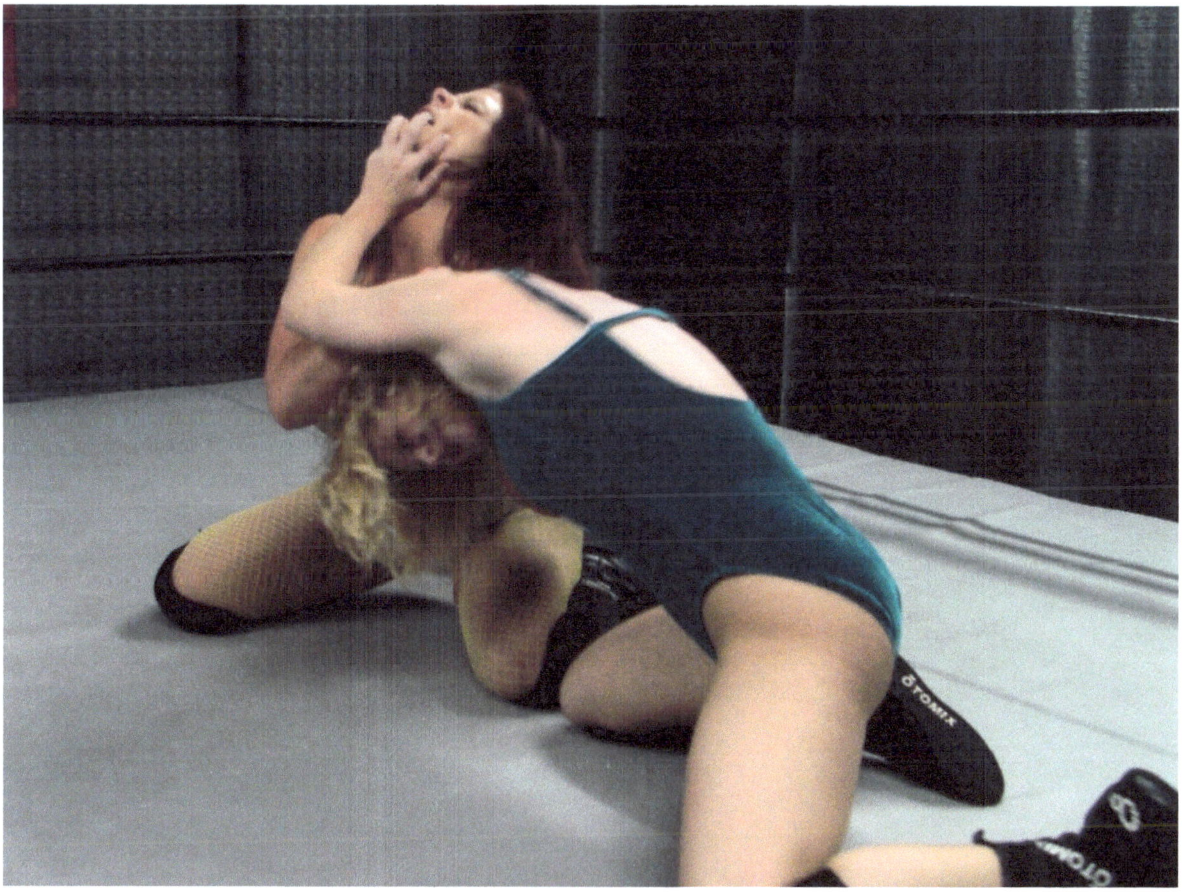

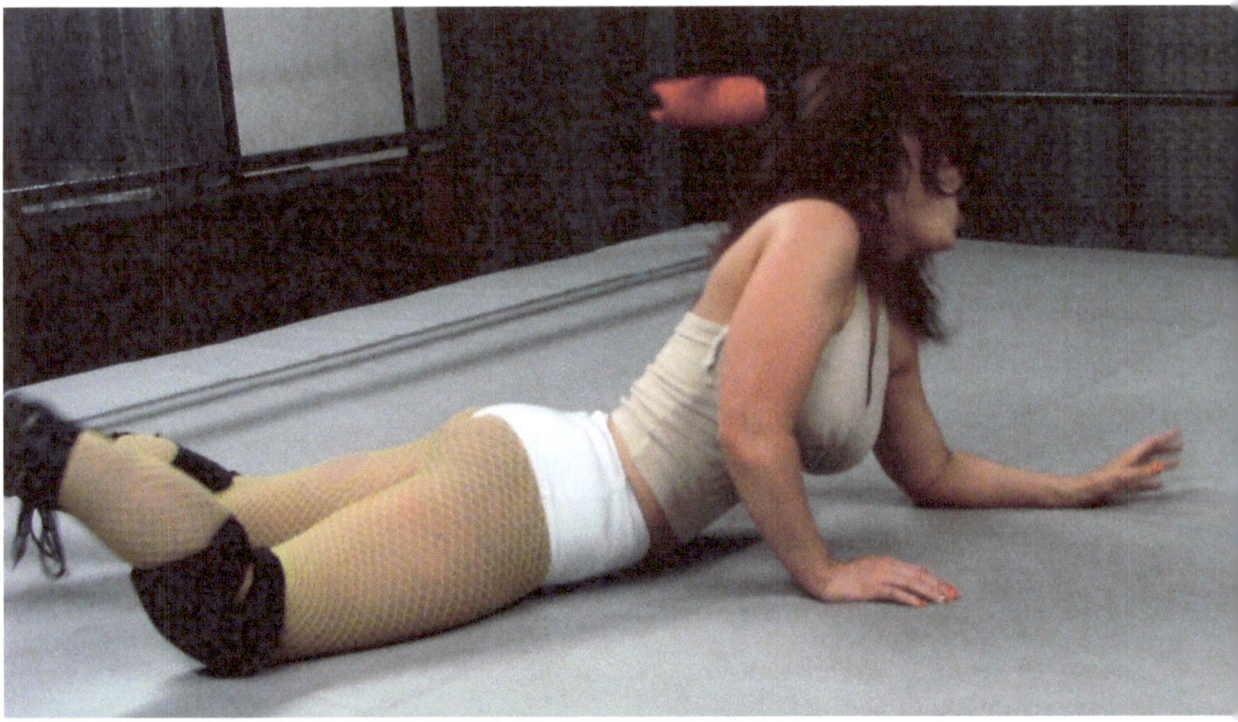

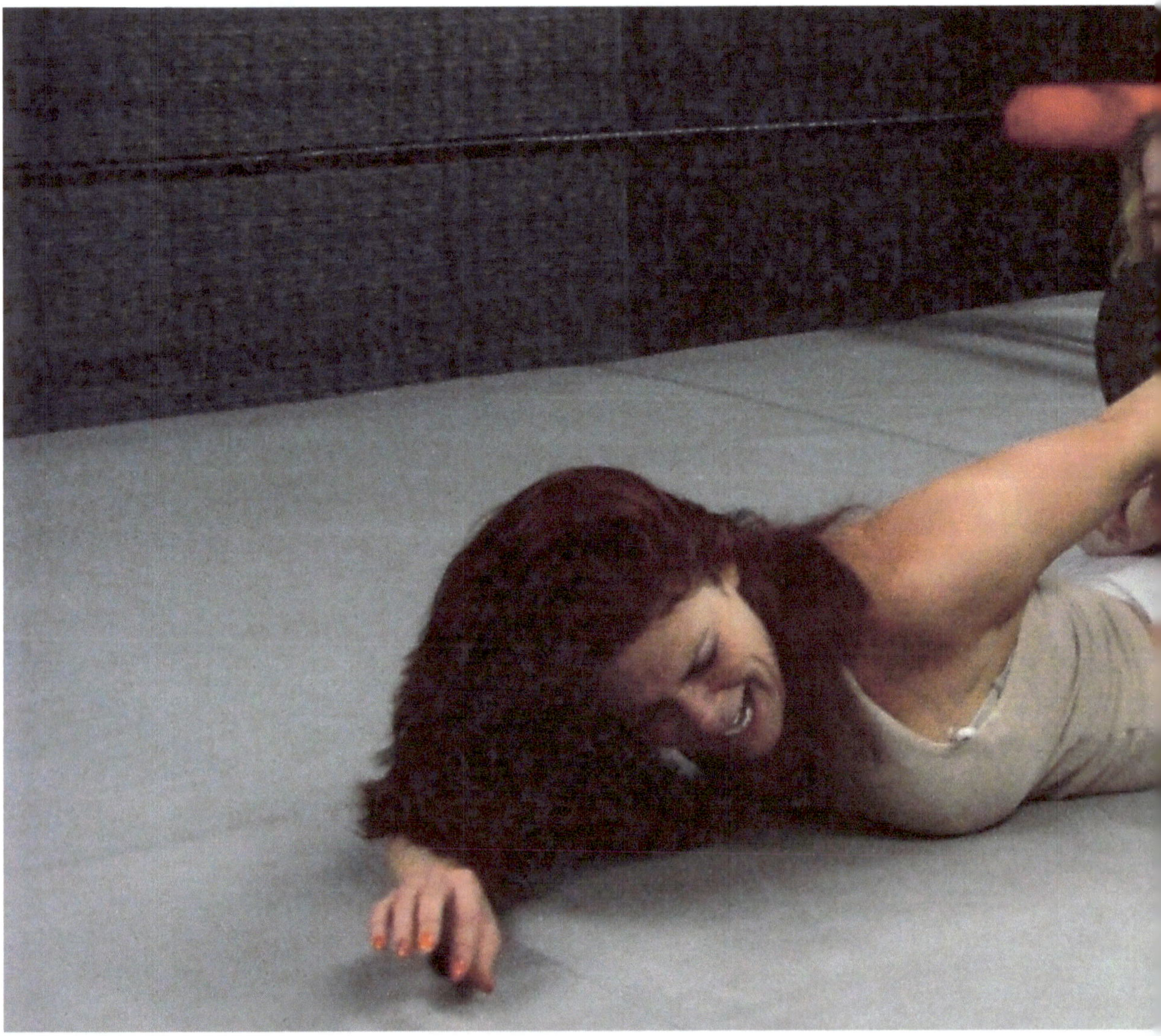

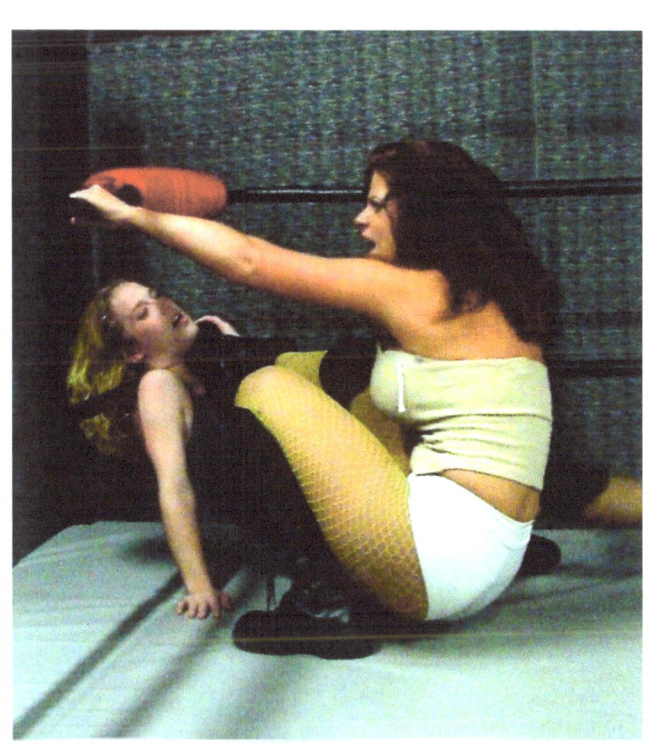

ALL GOOD THINGS

For nearly fifteen minutes these very sexy
young ladies go at it. That takes a lot of energy! Amazingly, it's Luscious Lee who finally gains a submission on her more experienced rival.

They'll meet again.

And Lee better be ready!

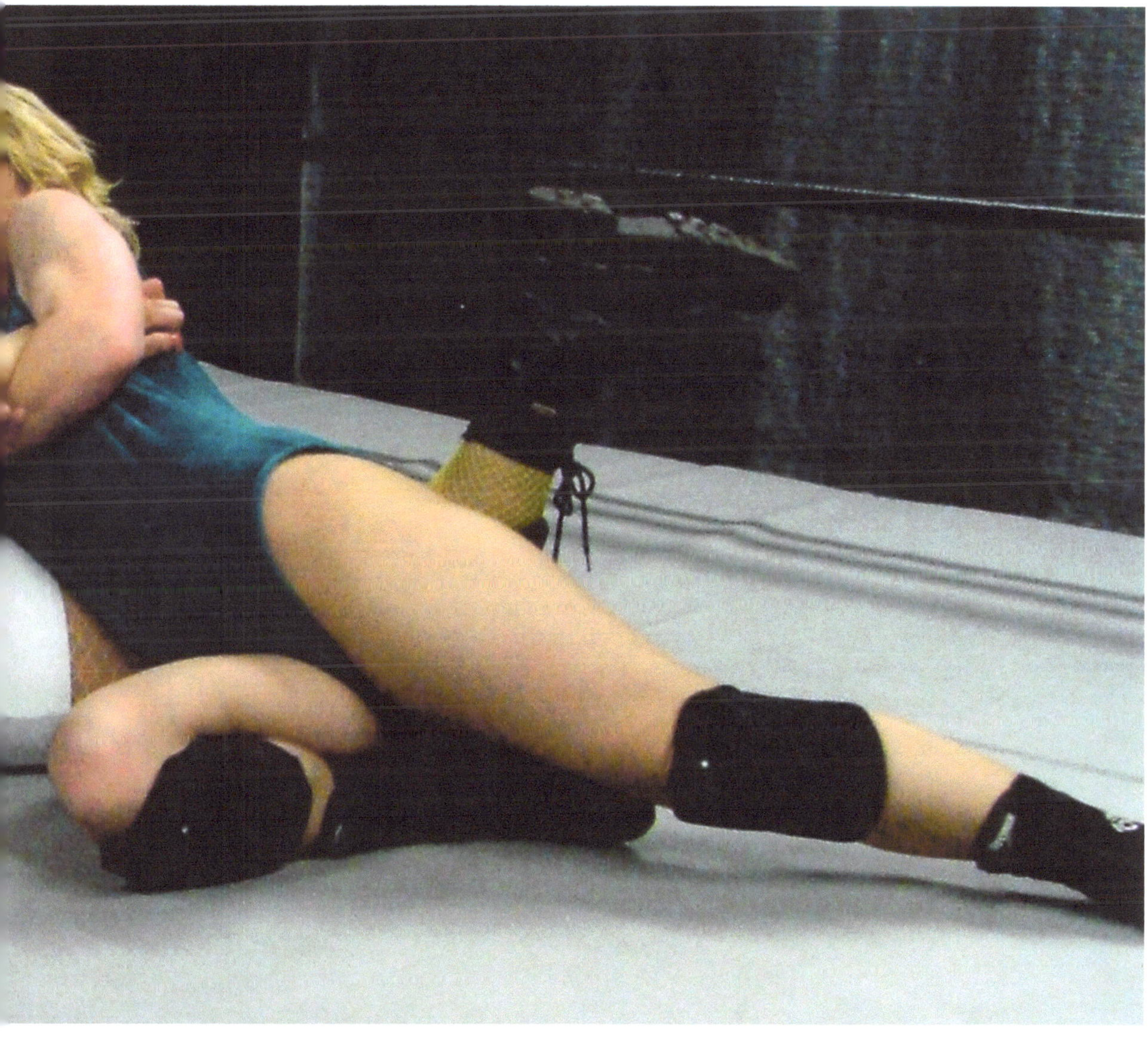

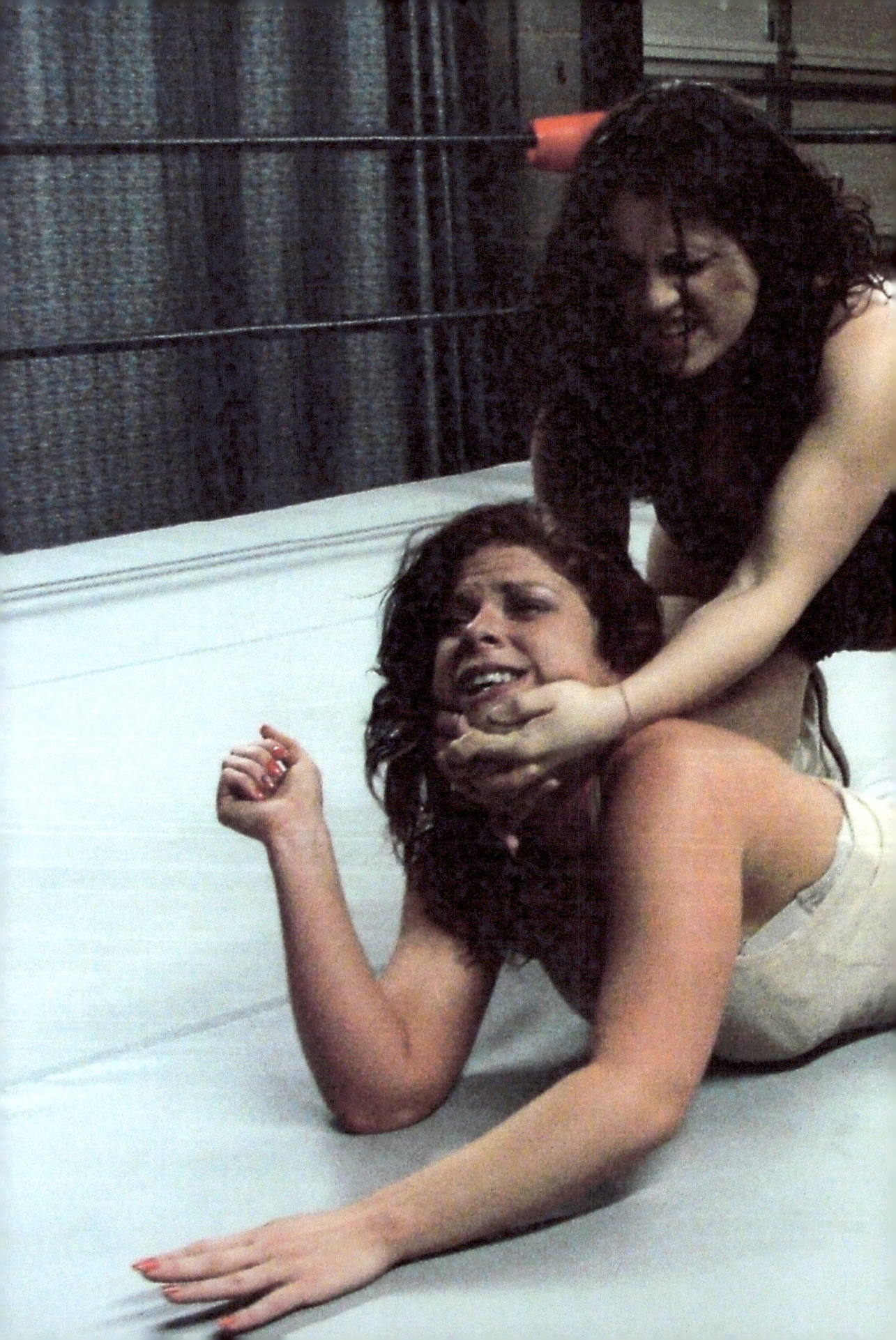

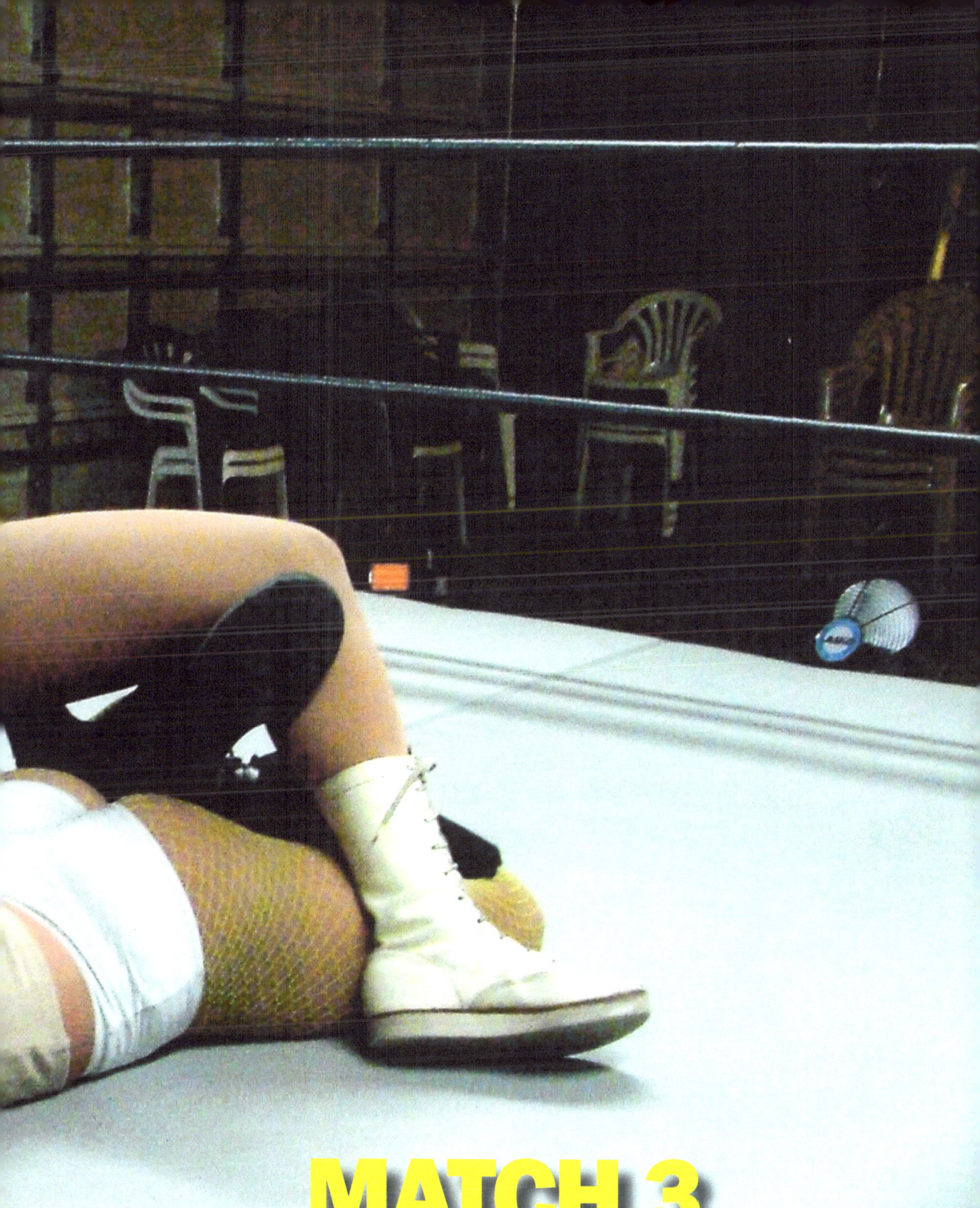

MATCH 3
PERSEPHONE VS LITTLE JEANNIE

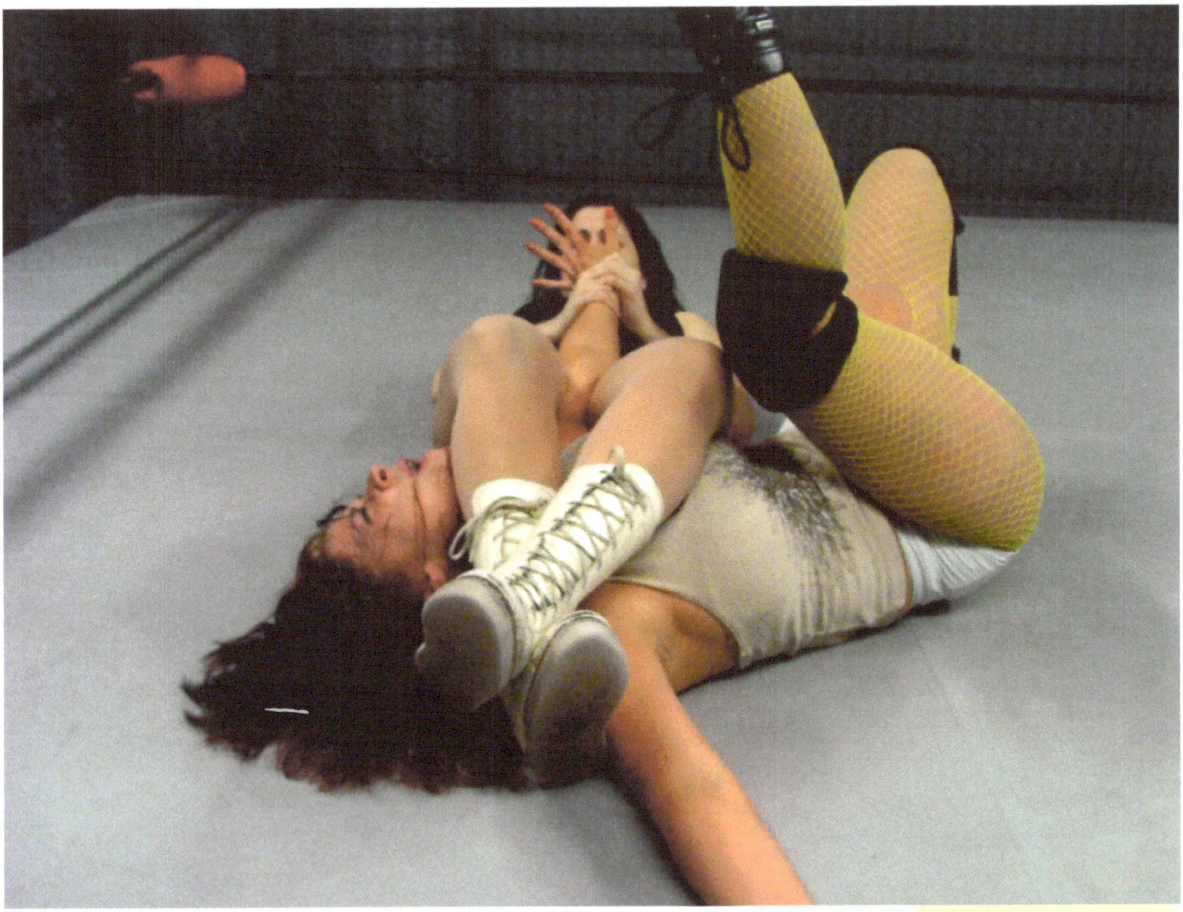

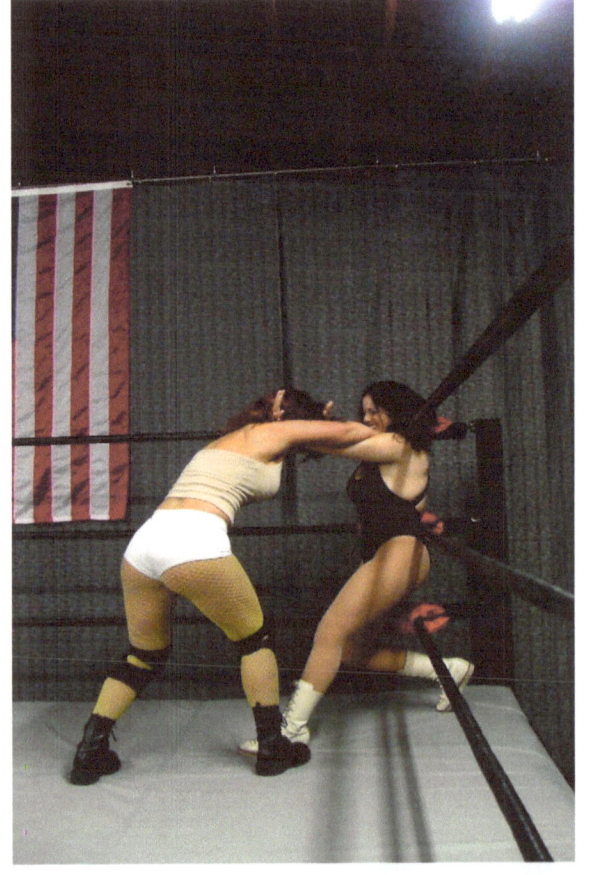

LITTLE JEANNE

This buxom brunette is a tough, no-nonsense grappler with years of experience across the country and Japan. Is she a good girl or a bad girl? Depending on who you talk to, the answer is "yes." Largely considered to hail from New York, she brings that attitude with her into the ring. Play nice with her, she'll play nice with you. Otherwise...

Jeanne knew little of Persephone, and many likened their skills and styles to be similar. Well, Persephone does make a little more noise when she wrestles. This private match for ThunderGirls harkened back to the "old school" days of womens' wrestling. They know holds. They know how to punish. But there can be only one winner.

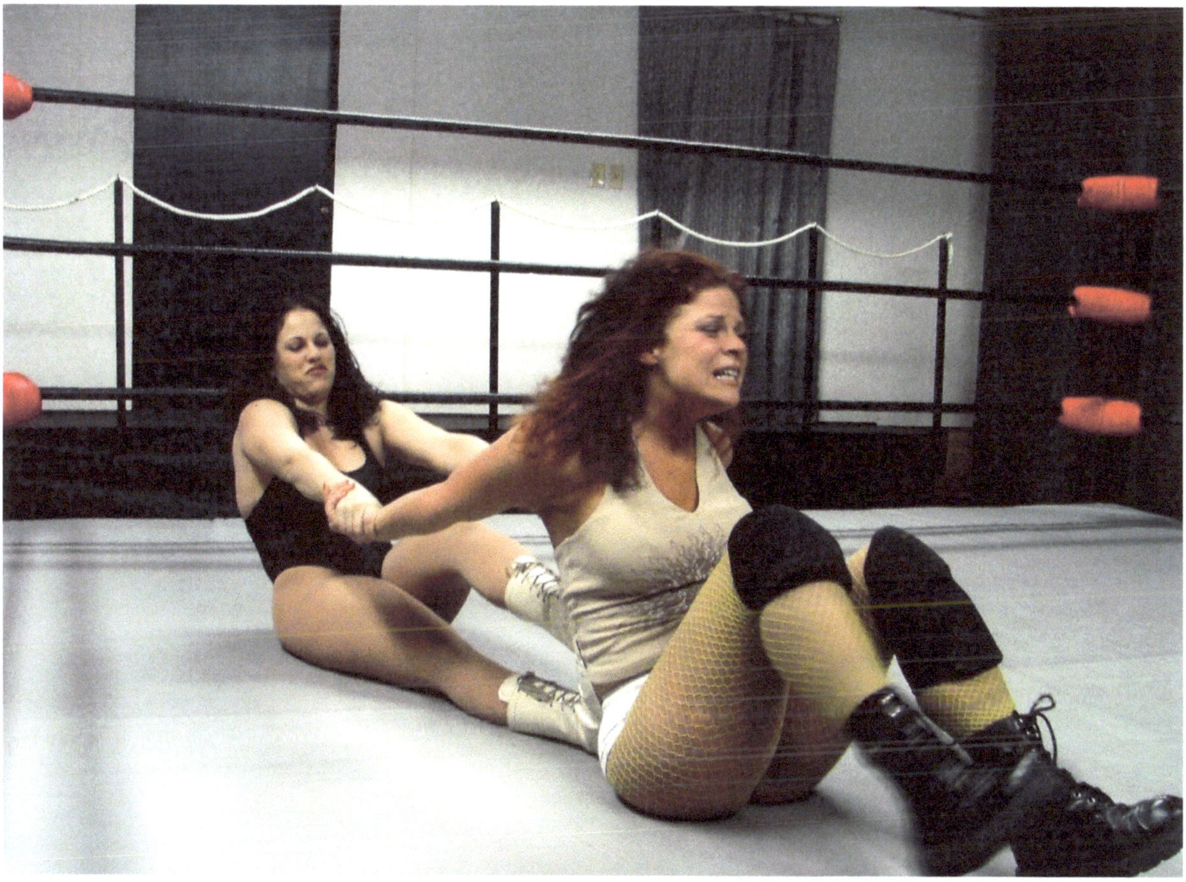

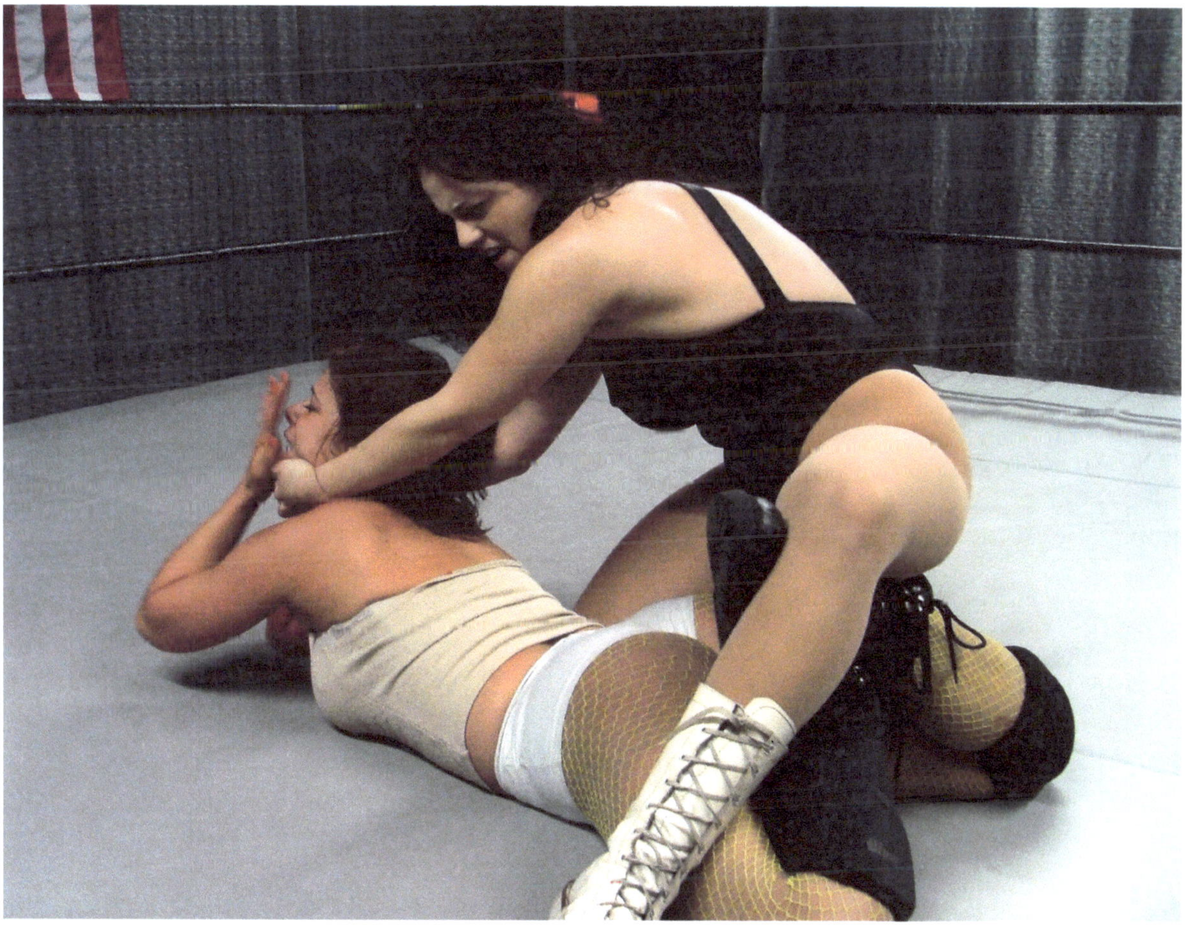

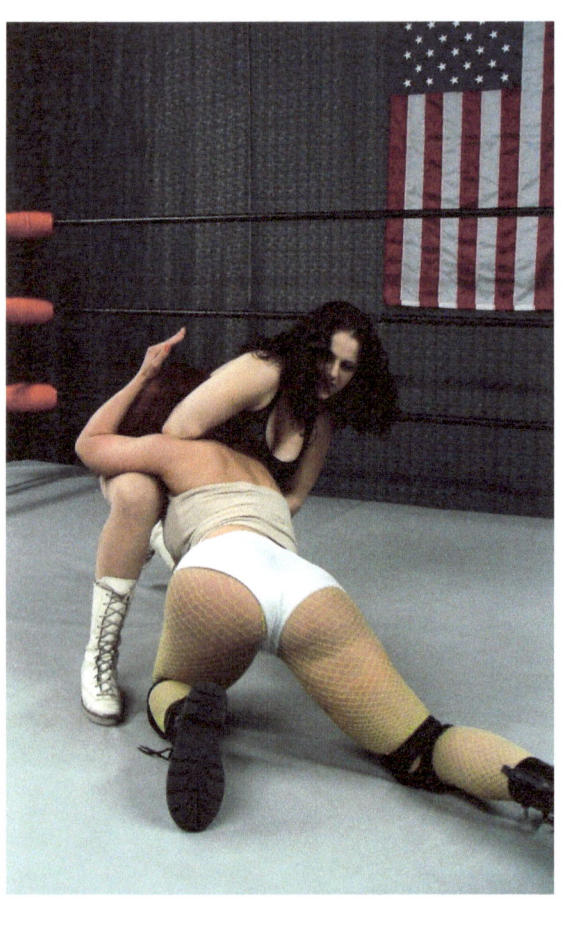

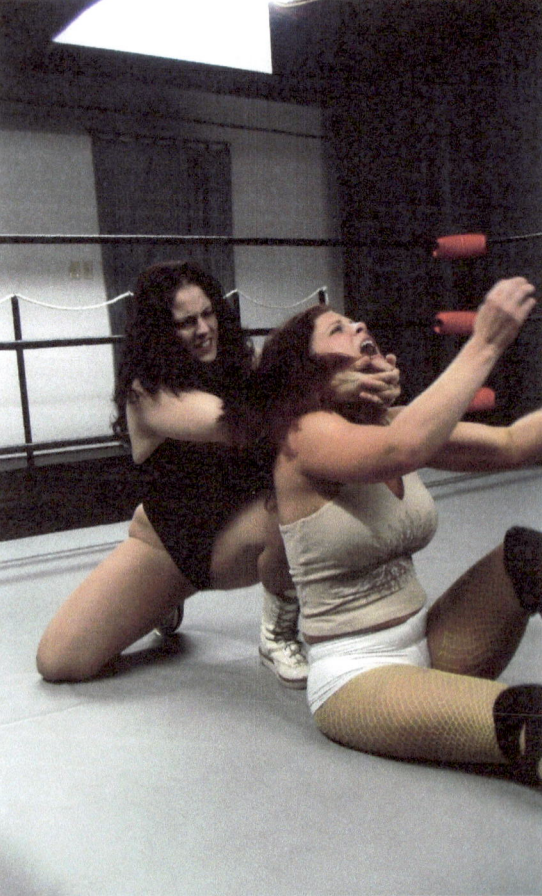

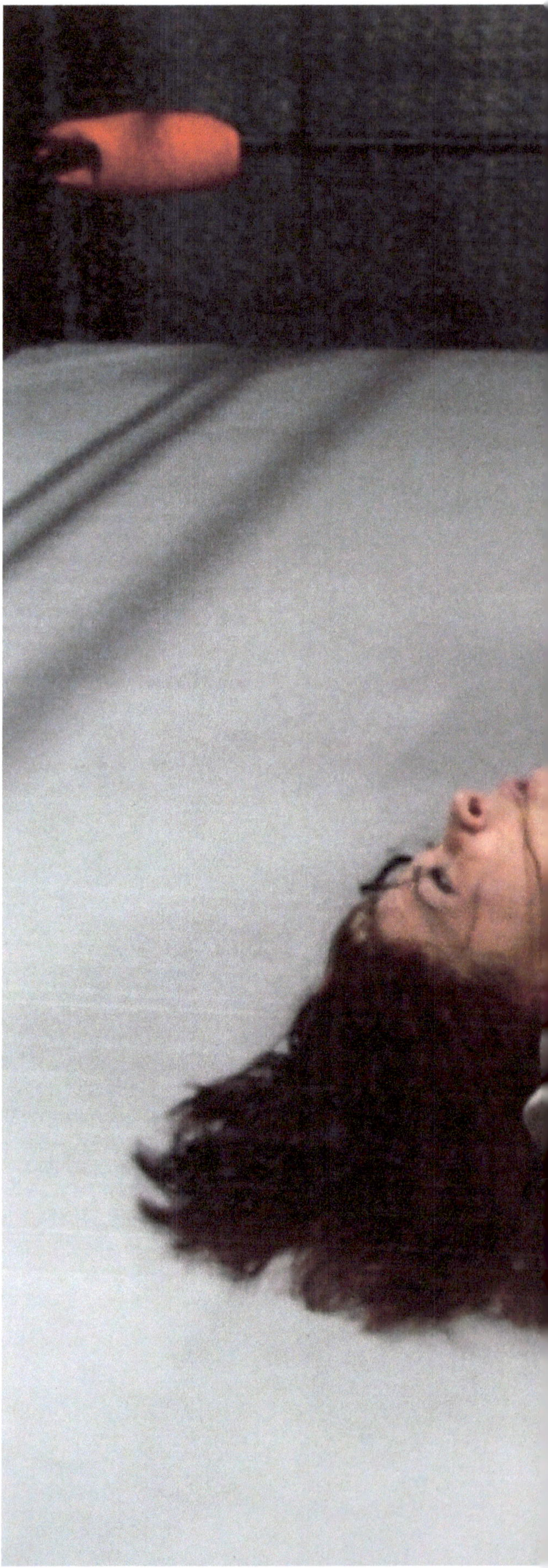

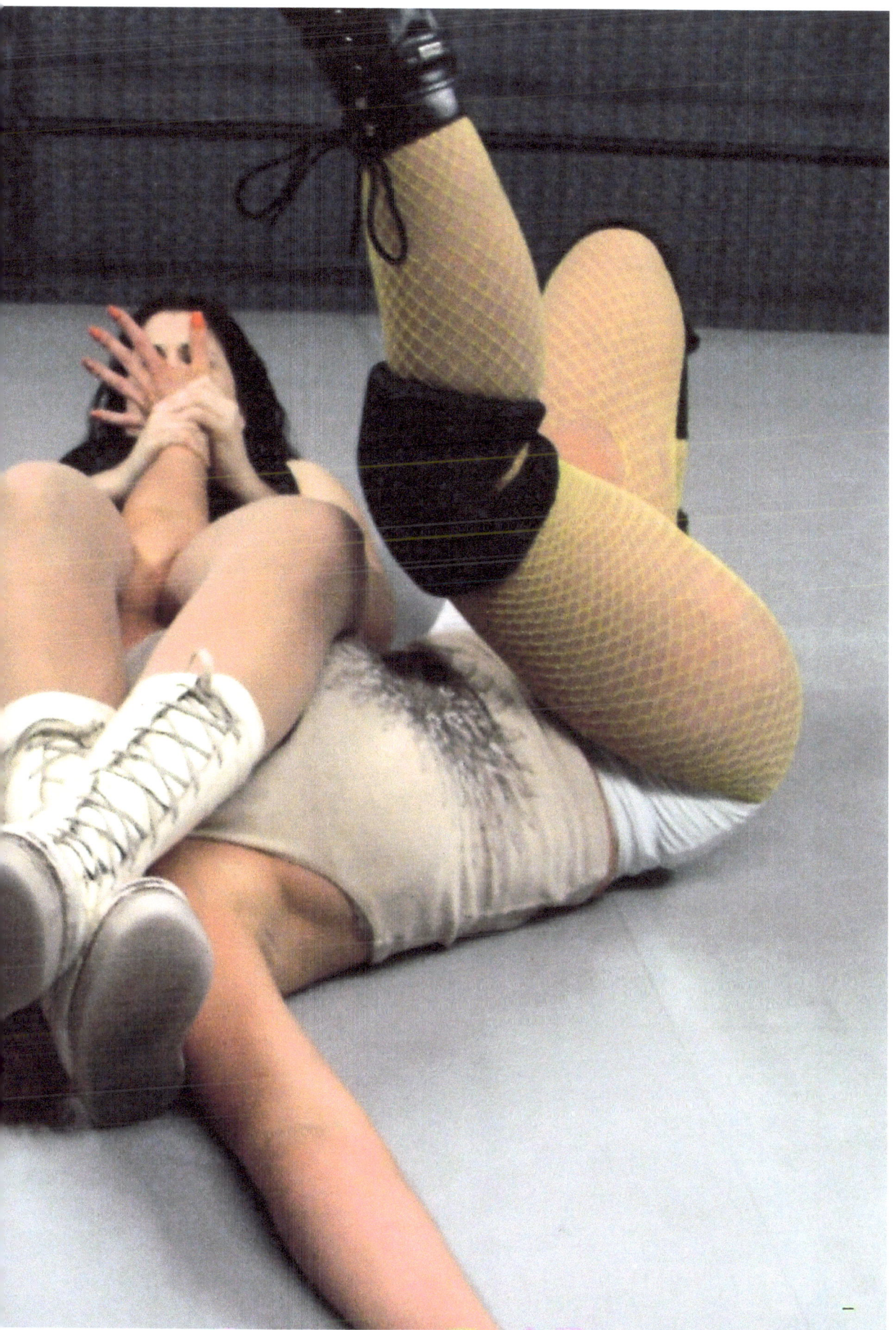

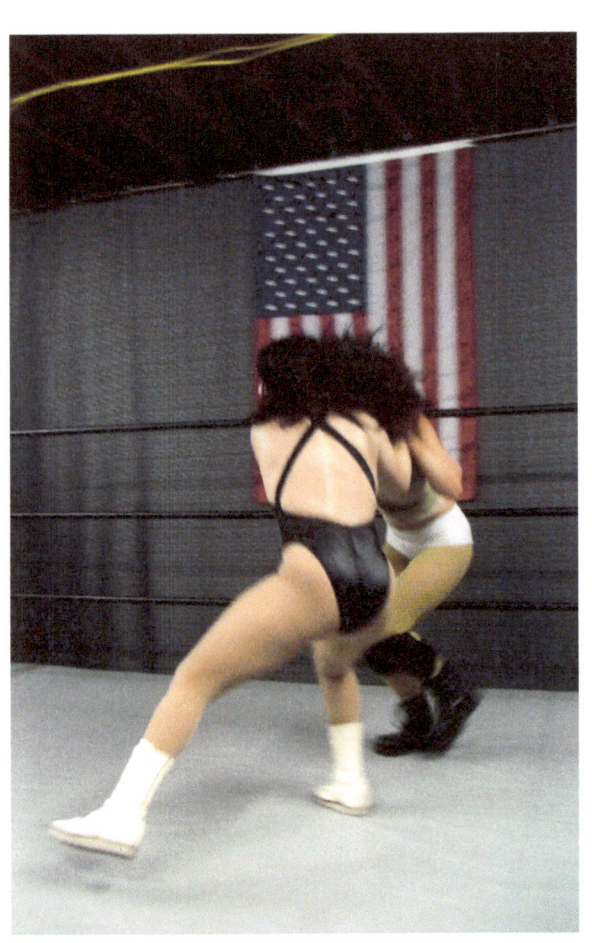
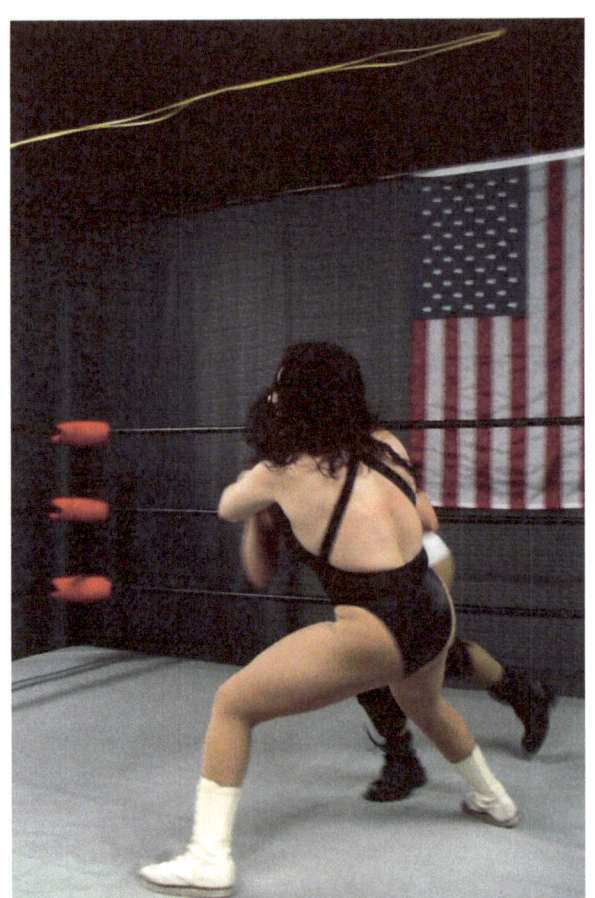
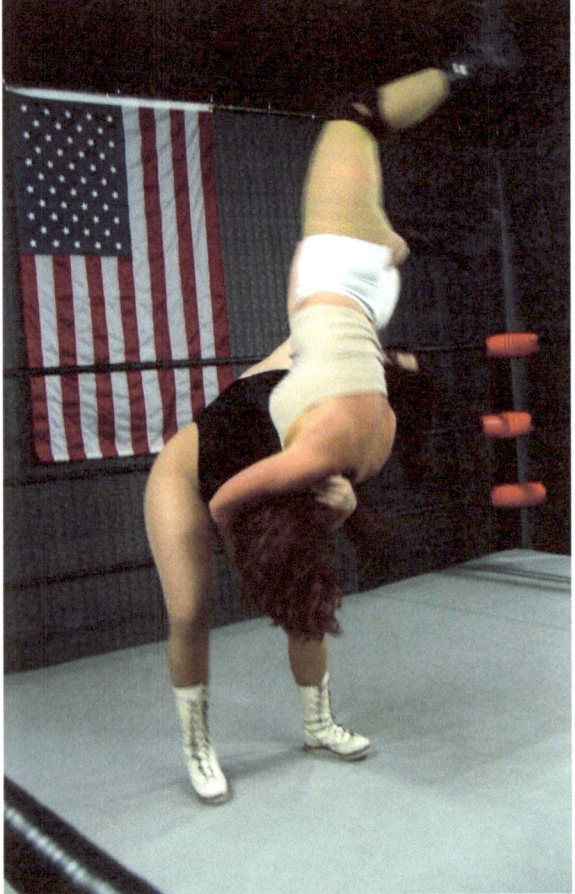
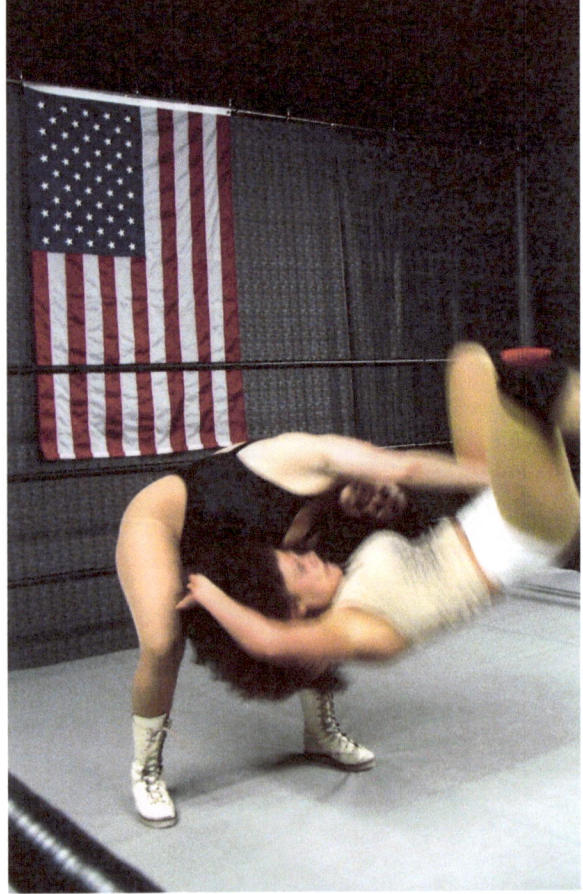

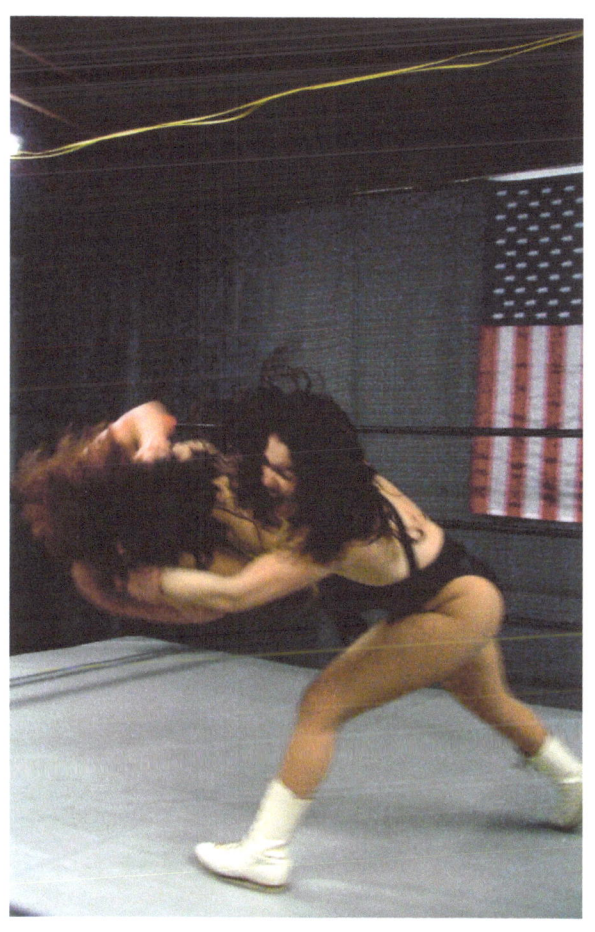

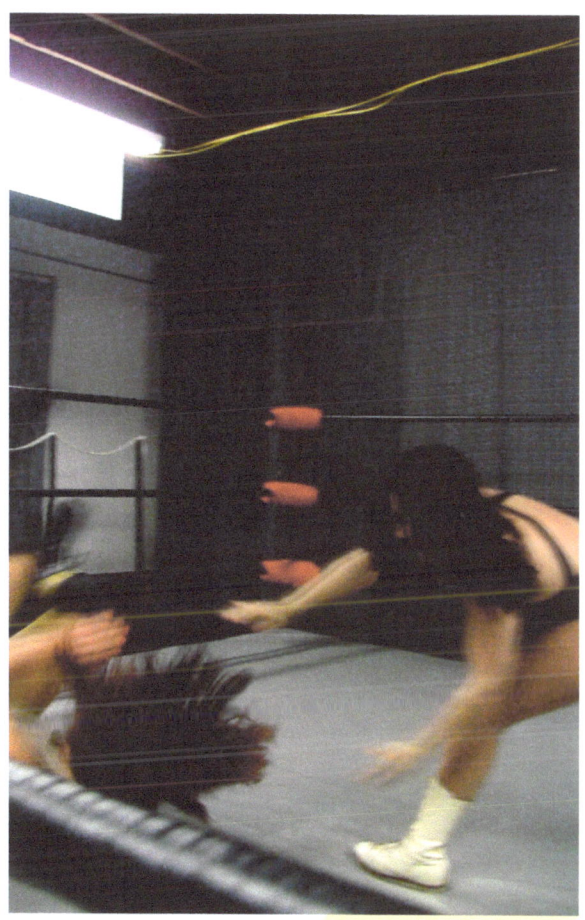

SLAM!

As you can see from these exciting images, these girls were all over the ring. They wanted to control, to toss, to bash, to punish.

And they succeeded. Persephone is a tough opponent, but Little Jeanne, as it turns out, is a little tougher.

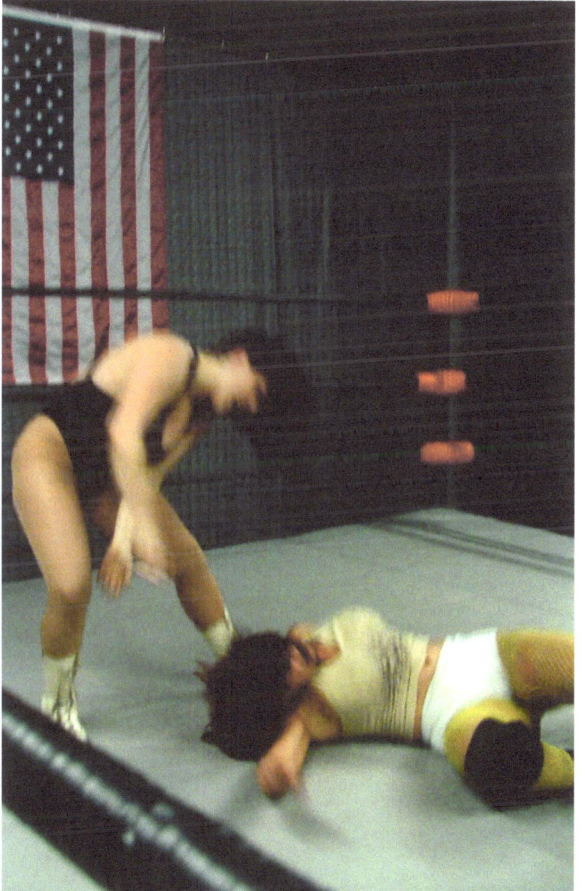

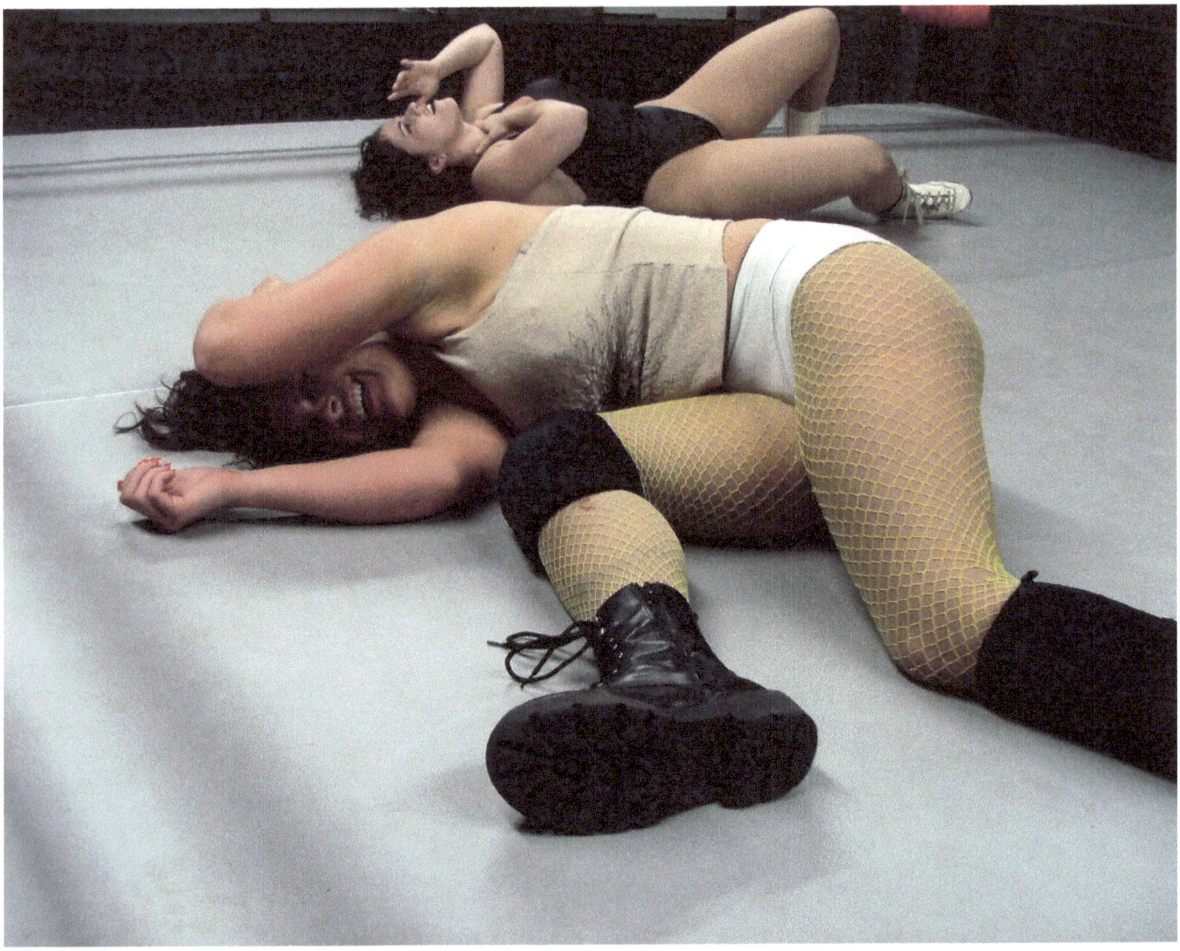

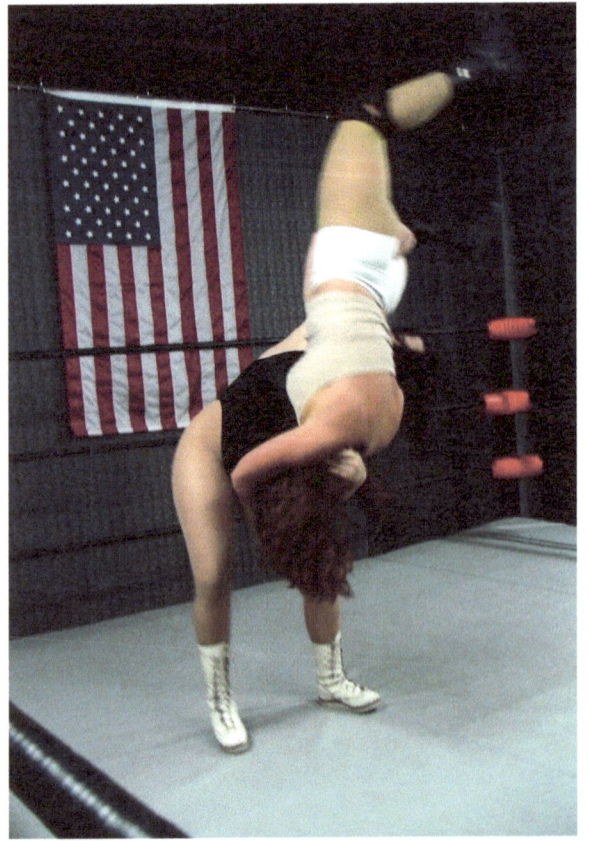

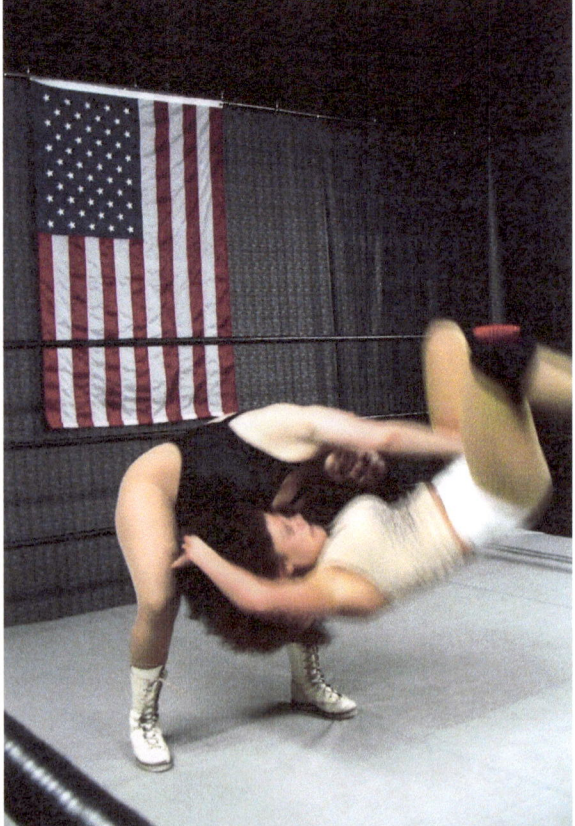

www.ingramcontent.com/pod-product-compliance
Lightning Source LLC
Chambersburg PA
CBHW050359180526
45159CB00005B/2076